SOUTHEAST ASIA, AN EMERGING CENTER OF WORLD INFLUENCE?

ECONOMIC AND RESOURCE CONSIDERATIONS

SOUTHEAST ASIA, AN EMERGING CENTER OF WORLD INFLUENCE?

Economic and Resource Considerations

Edited by

Wayne Raymond and K. Mulliner

Ohio University
Center for International Studies
Papers in International Studies
Southeast Asia Series No. 42

Library of Congress Card Catalog
Number: 76-620090

ISBN Number: 0-8214-0324-9

PREFACE

The Southeast Asia Studies Program at Ohio University hosted a symposium on the topic "Southeast Asia: An Emerging Center of World Influence?" on May 7 and 8, 1976. The papers in this volume represent the presentations of two of the panels in the symposium. It will surprise no one familiar with academic symposia that the question of Southeast Asia's emerging world influence is not definitively answered here, but exploration of the question provided ample opportunity for the contributors to analyze the important economic and resource variables which will determine the eventual answer.

In the Economic section, Professor Douglas Paauw places Southeast Asian economic growth in world and historical perspectives and identifies the divergencies among the growth rates of the separate nations. Professor Frank Golay offers sobering reminders that there are significant internal obstacles to achieving world economic power. He does see, however, regional cooperation as a potential route to world economic influence. Professor Castro looks at the question specifically in terms of the Association of Southeast Asian Nations (ASEAN). Dr. Lawrence Stifel's comments on the papers provide a stimulating overview.

Crucial to the prospects for economic growth is the development of natural resources. As Professor Paauw observes, the export of raw and processed resources is necessary to provide the import capacity needed for industrialization and modernization in Southeast Asia. In the Resource section, James Osborn looks at the relationship between resources and economic development in the ASEAN nations. Moving from this overview, Professor James Hafner explores the dilemma of resource exploitation and environmental preservation as perceived by different elements within the Thai social structure. Beyond the perceptual question in considering resources is the need to extend the benefits of a nation's resources to the less-affluent portions of the population. Professor Karl Pelzer examines Malaysia's Federal Land Development Authority as a modern response to this need. Drawing on his decades of experience and research in Southeast Asia, Professor Pelzer compares this current effort with earlier government-sponsored programs in the Philippines and the Netherlands East Indies.

The Appendices provide some of the statistical bases on which the contributors relied. The contributors are identified by their institutional affiliations in the Table of Contents.

* * * * * * * * * * *

In addition to the papers presented in this volume, the Symposium featured panels on the "Possibilities of Social Revolution in Southeast Asia," "Vietnam: One Year Later," "Strategies and Political Systems of Southeast Asia," "The Future of Southeast Asian Studies in the U.S.," and "Leadership Roles of Women in Southeast Asia." The latter two panels consisted of informal presentations and discussions. The panel on leadership roles of women featured four prominent Southeast Asian women brought to the United States by the national League of Women Voters and their participation was co-sponsored by the Athens chapter of the League.

In addition to the panels, Helen Castello (Pennsylvania State at Stroudsburg) presented a slide lecture on "Pagan before the Earthquake," and Gayl Ness (University of Michigan) provided a lecture and videotape on "Cadres and Capitalists: Varying Entrepreneurial Strategies in Generating Popular Participation (Family Planning in China and Thailand)." A highlight of the symposium was a Southeast Asian dinner served to 125 persons under the direction of Mrs. Ina Tirtonegoro of Athens.

The Symposium was chaired by the Director of the Southeast Asia Program at Ohio University, Professor Paul R. Deuster. William Frederick, Professor Paul W. van der Veur, and Professor Deuster developed the program for the Symposium. In keeping with another academic tradition, many of the details and arrangements which are essential to a successful gathering were handled by graduate students in the Southeast Asia Program. John Davis, Edward Dooley and Fred Keeler (with the assistance of Bernie Cleveland of the O. U. Workshops Office) labored at length in handling local arrangements and the innumerable details and changes. While the above shouldered the major organizational burdens, all of the graduate students (and even some undergraduates) in the Program willingly provided assistance and labor beyond reasonable expectations. All of them deserve special credit for their contributions.

K. Mulliner
Wayne Raymond

Southeast Asia Program
Center for International Studies
Ohio University
Athens, Ohio
March 1977

CONTENTS

Abbreviations

ASEAN - Association of Southeast Asian Nations, composed of Indonesia, Malaysia, The Philippines, Singapore and Thailand.

LDCs - Lesser Developed Countries.

NIEO - New International Economic Order.

THE ECONOMIC UNDERPINNINGS OF SOUTHEAST ASIA

Frank H. Golay

The power--actual and potential--of a nation or group of nations is the aggregate of diverse components. Power--political and economic--ultimately derives from the human resources of the nation state which are specified by such physical attributes as heads of population, age composition, the prevailing state of health, and by less tangible qualitative aspects of the human environment--the cultural heritage of attitudes and values, accumulated investment in the human factor, the shared perception of the national society, ideological commitment to the social organization, and so forth--which explain the elán of the national society. Members of the national society contribute to the power of the state by engaging in activities which increase material output, by foregoing present consumption in order to consume more in the future, by sustaining a transcendant loyalty to the nation state necessary to its defense, and by producing social innovations which ensure that the nation state responds to the felt needs of the national society and thereby retains the loyalty of its members.

A second ingredient of national power is the endowment of natural resources including climate, soils, configuration, topography, strategic aspects of location, as well as mineral deposits and forestry, fisheries and fauna resources. For the most part, natural resources must be produced by the application of existing economic resources to such tasks as clearing, leveling and terracing land to bring it into agricultural production. Mineral, forestry and fisheries resources must be produced in similar fashion. In other cases, human labor and existing capital resources are combined with features of the physical environment to produce improvements in transportation which facilitate economic integration and specialization and thereby contribute to improved resource productivity which augments national power. Similarly, the application of existing scientific knowledge and human resources to technological advance may be required to transform passive natural resources into economic resources by developing new applications for such resources in production and consumption. The economic resources which buttress power in Southeast Asia today, for the most part, had to await the development of steel ships and steam propulsion.

The third in the familiar triumvirate of productive resources, the stock of capital, is also an essential ingredient of national power, particularly when the concept of capital is broadened to include intangible capital embodied in human resources and the stock of knowledge which may be the most productive of all forms of capital. The role of the human factor in the accumulation of capital is self-evident; the stock of capital of any society reflects the application of existing economic resources to the production of capital resources by past generations of that society.

Assessments of Western observers of the natural resource endowment of Southeast Asia, with few exceptions, have been exaggerated. For example, probably no study of Indonesia or the Dutch East Indies appearing prior to 1960 neglected to refer to the "richness" of the resources of this territory. Initial assessments of this kind reflected incomplete and faulty knowledge as well as conventional wisdom concerning the "gains" to be realized from trade in the products of tropical Southeast Asia. In the nineteenth and early twentieth centuries, such assessments were supported by the range of minerals and commercial crops that were beginning to be exported from Southeast Asia in significant quantities--gold, silver, tin, petroleum, copper, iron ore, tungsten, chromite, nickel, manganese, coal, forest products, sugar, coffee, coconut products, rubber, abaca, and so forth, as well as the rapidly growing export surpluses of rice from Burma, Thailand, and the Indochinese peninsula.

Current assessments of the resource potential of Southeast Asia are more modest and more realistic as they have been tempered by the rapid growth of population in the region. Today there is widespread awareness of population growth as the major constraint upon the efforts of the states in the area to improve the proportions in which the human factor is combined with producible resources--capital and natural--which historically has been the principal source of increase in human productivity. Limits to the frontier of land suitable for cultivation to present crops and using existing techniques appear more imminent than they did a quarter century ago when the population of the region was only half its present size. In a few prominent cases, high grade resources have been exploited to the point of exhaustion. This is the case of the high grade chromite and iron ore deposits which contributed to Philippine export earnings in the past, as well as the petroleum deposits of Burma, and the teak resources of Burma and Thailand.

Another factor supporting a relatively cautious assessment of the economic underpinnings of Southeast Asia is the relative shortage of fuel resources in the area. No metallurgical coal is being produced in Southeast Asia although good quality anthracite coal is mined in North Vietnam. Petroleum production is presently concentrated in Sumatra and in the Borneo states bordering the South China Sea, although exploration is underway or projected throughout the region and the fuel outlook may change abruptly in the future.

When we turn to examination of the contribution of the stock of producible capital--tangible and intangible--to the power potential of Southeast Asia, a sober assessment is in order. Levels of per capita and aggregate income are low in the states of the region and therefore the margin of income over consumption which can be devoted to capital accumulation is small. The infrastructure of social investment in the region must be appraised as no more than adequate and because it reflects political considerations it is frequently maldistributed. Governments in the region are under heavy pressure to expand social services and bureaucratic employment which will encroach upon the capacity to add to the stock of social capital. Money and capital market institutions, both those of the indigenous market as well as those supporting modern activities in foreign and domestic trade and manufacturing, are well developed, but the role to be played by financial intermediation in raising the level of savings is constrained by the low level of real income prevailing in the area.

The states of Southeast Asia are well-endowed with populations which are growing rapidly although qualitative aspects of these populations do not support optimism in assessing their power potential. High levels of fertility in conjunction with rapidly falling mortality have resulted in relatively unproductive populations as the proportion of population under fifteen years is approaching one-half in most states in the area Productivity of labor is low and underemployment of the work force, both in the countryside and in the urban environment, is widespread. Growth in population currently is outstripping the rate at which nonagricultural employment opportunities materialize and the growth in average real income, while respectable by historical standards, does not prevent further widening of the gap between levels of real income maintained in the region and the industrialized world.

It is a "fact of life" for the states of Southeast Asia that they are "small powers" although not in terms of population, as Indonesia is the sixth most populous country of the world and the population of the region presently exceeds that of North America and is growing at a more rapid rate. In terms of area, moreover, most of the states of the region would fall in the middle range of countries. States relatively small in terms of power, by definition have few strategic options and the foreign policies of such states tend to be distinguished by historical continuity. It is in this sense that the states of Southeast Asia--with the exceptions of Indonesia and Vietnam--fall into this category.

If these states are "small powers," does the possibility exist that the region as a whole aggregates to world power status? The answer to this question at present must be a qualified "no" as there is an imponderable factor in the existing situation that could reverse this assessment. The fighting ceased in the Indochinese peninsula only a year ago with North Vietnam the clear victor in a war of attrition with a major world power. That society has emerged from a prolonged trial of arms tightly knit, resourceful and flexible, and with a clear capability to pursue regional objectives beyond the Indochinese nations. This is not to predict the integration of the Southeast Asian region into a world power under North Vietnamese hegemony in the foreseeable future, but this possibility cannot be dismissed.

Concern for Vietnamese actions either alone or in conjunction with an intrusive world power is likely to sustain efforts on the part of the "open" economies of the region--Thailand, Malaysia, Singapore, Indonesia, and the Philippines--to explore the contribution which regional cooperation and integration can make to the power and security of these states in the uncertain international environment in which they find themselves. What are the prospects that these states can achieve major power status through regional cooperation and integration?

The burden of Southeast Asian history is a formidable obstacle to regionalism. The area has been much fought over and migrations of populations have dispossessed, and in some cases decimated, other populations. Impressive monuments--Angkor, Ayutia, Pagan, Borobudur--confirm that civilizations flourished, expanded, encountered reverses, and were displaced or extinguished. In the case of the mainland of Southeast Asia, which escaped colonization by the West until the nineteenth century, the emnity of the Burmese and Thais is a recent and strong memory. Similarly, the traditional animosities between Thais and Khmers, Khmers and Vietnamese, and Thais and Vietnamese, which were renewed by the French in extending and maintaining their rule in Indochina, remain close to the surface. In establishing her rule Spain encountered little resistance in converting the peoples in the northern and central parts of the Philippine archipelago, but Islam, which had captured the minds of

Filipinos in the Sulu archipelago and in southwestern Mindanao, proved inpenetrable to Spanish proselytizing. The intermittent warfare and piratical raiding of the succeeding centuries fueled a lasting animosity between the Christian north and the Muslim south in the Philippines which is blazing today.

The island empires based upon the strategic importance of the Straits of Malacca flourished and exercised hegemony before the coming of the Europeans and left a residue of memories which serve to maintain anxieties and suspicions that are latent today. This legacy was confirmed by the period of Konfrontasi in the 1960s when the peoples of the Malay peninsula responded vigorously to an Indonesian initiative which revived fears that the Javanese people would reassert strategic dominance of the region adjacent to the Straits of Malacca. Similarly, the assertion of the Philippine claim to Sabah stirred memories of Muslim empires in the area bordering the Sulu Sea, Makassar Strait and North Borneo and acerbated tensions in the wider region. Peripheral to the warfare in Indochina were small-scale vendettas between Khmer and Vietnamese, and between Lao/Thai and Vietnamese which have roots extending through the history of the area.

A second major obstacle to Southeast Asia regionalism is the colonial legacy of political and economic isolation which has characterized the states of the region. The industrial revolution in northwestern Europe followed closely by the technological breakthrough represented by steam propulsion and steel ships was attended by a comparable change in colonial policy. Mercantilism was abandoned for *laissez faire* capitalism which, in conjunction with direct rule, hastened the development of the colonies as markets for the manufactures of the industrial West and as sources of supply of tropical foodstuffs and industrial raw materials.

Although economic liberalism was extended to colonial policy by the British and the Dutch, the political and investment relationships between these countries and their colonies ensured that the trade of the latter would be concentrated in exchanges with the colonial power. The late entrants in the race of industrialization and for empire--France and the United States--were more aggressive in monopolizing the trade of their colonies by mutual trade preferences. As a result, the modest economic development taking place in the region was a process in which the colonies "faced outward, turning their backs to their neighbors." Colonial development produced little regional specialization and integration and this pattern has persisted to the present.

A related obstacle to regionalism in Southeast Asia is the structure of manufacturing development resulting from the industrial development strategy common to the countries of the area. The major change represented by independence was the substitution of government by nationals for colonial rule, and the new governments were confronted by the necessity to make good on the promises of successful nationalist movements. One such promise was a commitment to transform the colonial-type economies by industrial development, and each country initially sought to hasten this process by recourse to directly productive public enterprise. The results of this industrialization strategy proved uniformly disappointing, however, and over time the states of the area turned to "import substitution" to induce manufacturing development based upon indigenous participation and the internal market. Such a strategy typically was implemented by high levels of protection maintained by tariffs in conjunction with currency overvaluation, subsidization of manufacturing activities by allocation of foreign exchange and credit and remission of tariffs and internal taxes, and limitation of competitive pressures by strict control over access to markets and resources.

While the experience with industrial efforts has varied widely over the area, manufacturing output has increased generally. The inadequacies of "import substitution" as a strategy, however, led to its abandonment in the extreme form dependent upon currency overvaluation and the modest expansion in manufacturing taking place in Southeast Asia today is sustained, for the most part, by high levels of protection.

Because industrial development is dependent upon protection, manufacturing output has tended to reflect historical patterns of imports of manufactures. As a result, output is concentrated in consumer goods and relatively simple industrial products--processed foods, clothing, footwear, textiles, petroleum refining, rubber manufactures, simple metal fabrication, automobile assembly, pharmaceuticals, simple industrial chemicals and miscellaneous manufactures--a pattern which varies little from state to state. The essence of regional economic integration is the division of labor, i.e., specialization within the region, but manufacturing development in Southeast Asia has not resulted in regional integration, but the opposite. National manufacturing interests heavily subsidized and sheltered from competition will persist as an obstacle to economic regionalism.

Because of these factors, regionalism has had a checkered history in Southeast Asia. In the early postwar years, the states of the area were undeviating in their support of the United Nations and the role of that forum in bringing into existence an international public motivated to eliminate the last vestiges of colonialism. Regional unity within the United Nations also was sustained by a shared perception of the role of that institution in enlarging the sovereignty of amall states through a viable system of collective security.

With the collapse of Nationalist resistance in China and the subsequent war in Korea, the faith of a number of Southeast Asian societies in collective security was shaken but not enough to prevent regional unity in the Bandung Conference of 1955. With important leadership from Sukarno and U Nu, this meeting of leaders of less developed countries took the first important step in organizing these states into a viable bloc which has maintained impressive unity and gained influence in the turbulent years since its founding. Cold War tensions in the area of eastern Asia which culminated in the prolonged Vietnamese war, as well as concern for the regional ambitions of Sukarno's Indonesia, subsequently eroded the regional unity of purpose evident in the common opposition to colonialism and regional cooperation in efforts to preserve substantive neutralism in the area.

Within this overall pattern of change, efforts to explore the potentialities of Southeast Asian regionalism have persisted, and interactions between Southeast Asians in positions of leadership have expanded steadily. Although none of these efforts has included all the states of the region, they were never intended to be exclusive but provided for the accession of nonparticipating states.

The initial attempt to bring into existence a purely regional grouping was the Association of Southeast Asia (ASA) which was founded in 1961 by the Philippines, Thailand, and Malaya. Activities of ASA were interrupted in 1963 when the Philippines advanced its claim to North Borneo and diplomatic relations between the Philippines and Malaysia were suspended. Although diplomatic relations between the two countries were resumed in 1965, the activities of ASA did not flourish thereafter. During its brief existence the ASA held *ad hoc* consultations on regional issues and maintained continuing joint committees and working parties.

In 1967, the Association of Southeast Asian Nations (ASEAN) was formed by the ASA states--Malaysia, the Philippines, and Thailand--plus Indonesia and Singapore. ASEAN has remained active since its founding and has acquired stature as a forum for consultation among the participating states.

The modest accomplishments of these efforts to expand regional cooperation to a substantial degree have reflected the limited economic integration within the area. Intraregional trade accounts for a relatively small fraction of the total trade of the states of the area. For the three years 1970 through 1972, intraregional exports of the ten Southeast Asia countries for which data are available, averaged $1,681 million dollars annually, and accounted for 23.5 per cent of the global exports of these countries (see Table 1). The shares of intraregional exports in total exports varied from a high of 83 per cent in the case of Laos, which accounted for less than one per cent of the exports of the area, to a low of two per cent in the case of the Philippines. Intraregional trade was dominated by Malaysia and Singapore which accounted for 48 per cent of the global exports of the region and provided just over two-thirds of intraregional exports. Mutual trade between Malaysia and Singapore averaged $765 million annually or 45 per cent of intraregional exports. In contrast, Indonesia, the Philippines and Thailand, which accounted for 46 per cent of global exports of the region, provided only one-quarter of intraregional exports.

The modest level of economic integration in Southeast Asia indicated by intraregional exports must be scaled down substantially when account is taken of the volume of regional exports that are transhipped through Singapore with only marginal value added by processing or packaging. Thanks to its strategic location and natural harbor, Singapore developed as an _entrepôt_, assembling the produce of the region for shipment to the West and distributing the manufactures received in return.

For the three years 1970-1972, export shipments from Singapore of foods and raw materials produced in Southeast Asia averaged some $625 million, including shipments of natural rubber valued at $332 million and of petroleum and related products of some $120 million (see Table 2). In view of the small area and the extensive industrial development and urbanization of Singapore, no significant exportable surpluses of these commodities could have resulted from their production on Singapore Island, although substantial value was added by petroleum refining and minor incremental value was added by the trading and packaging of primary products shipped through Singapore. It is not possible to determine the proportion of raw materials exported by the region to Singapore which were retained by that country, but, except in the case of petroleum, this ratio was not high for the commodities listed.

When the value of Singapore's exports of the produce of Southeast Asia during 1970-1972 is compared to the total of the intraregional exports of the area of $1.7 billion, it seems reasonably clear that intraregional exports retained within the area may have accounted for no more than two-thirds of all intraregional exports.

Retained intraregional exports, therefore, probably did not exceed one-sixth of the global exports of the area.

In assessing the economic integration within the region, it also is necessary to take into consideration the very high proportion of foods and raw materials in intraregional exports. For the period 1963-1965 for which data are available, intraregional exports of foods and raw materials of eight Southeast Asia countries averaged $698 million or two-thirds of the intraregional exports of these countries (see Table 3). If it were possible to eliminate from the exports of Singapore (which accounted for almost one-half of intraregional exports of the eight countries tabulated) the transhipment to regional states of manufactures from the outside world, the proportion of retained intraregional exports other than foods and raw materials would be a minor fraction--perhaps five per cent--of exports from Southeast Asian states.

Meaningful economic integration requires a specialization within the region which spreads across the spectrum of goods traded from foods and raw materials through capital equipment and high technology manufactures. Southeast Asia has yet to progress beyond a preliminary stage of regional economic integration. As a result, over the foreseeable future, the power potential represented by the resources--human, natural and capital, tangible and intangible--found in Southeast Asia is unlikely to be augmented substantially by regional cooperation and integration. It follows from this assessment that the economic underpinnings supporting Southeast Asian aspirations for world power status are, in the opinion of the writer, no more than minimal.

Table 1

Intraregional Export Trade in Southeast Asia, 1970-1972
(Annual Average $U.S. Million)

Exporting Country	Country of Destination										Total Intraregional Exports	Global Exports	Ratio of Intraregional to Global Exports (%)
	Brunei	Burma	Cambodia	Indonesia	Laos	Malaysia	Philippines	Singapore	Thailand	S. Vietnam			
Brunei[a]	-	1.5	-	.1	-	62.2	4.3	8.1	5.1	-	81.3	141.2	57.6%
Burma	-	-	-	3.5	-	4.1	2.7	10.1	-	-	20.4	118.3	17.2
Cambodia	-	-	-	-	-	-	-	1.1	.1	1.3	2.5	16.0	15.6
Indonesia	-	.2	-	-	-	49.5	19.8	149.4	.3	.2	219.4	1344.1	16.3
Laos	-	-	-	-	-	2.4	-	.2	1.9	-	4.5	5.4	83.3
Malaysia	9.0	3.9	-	10.8	-	-	29.4	367.1	17.4	1.4	439.0	1663.0	26.4
Philippines	.6	-	-	2.9	-	1.0	-	10.3	3.1	3.6	21.5	1093.9	2.0
Singapore	34.1	4.7	9.5	74.7[b]	-	398.0	10.1	-	59.8	115.4	706.3	1804.4	39.1
Thailand	-	-	5.7	21.1	22.1	43.0	16.3	67.0	-	10.6	185.8	874.1	21.3
S. Vietnam	-	-	-	-	-	-	-	.4	-	-	.4	7.9	5.1
	43.7	10.3	15.2	113.1	22.1	560.2	82.6	613.7	87.7	132.5	1681.1	7168.3	23.5%

Source: U.N., Yearbook of International Trade Statistics, 1974

[a] Average for 1971-1972

[b] Imports from Singapore reported by Indonesia

[c] "-", either no exports recorded, or the recorded value of exports was less than $50,000

Table 2

The Entrepôt Trade of Singapore In Foods and Raw Materials Produced In Southeast Asia, 1970-1972

(Exports f.o.b., Annual Average $U.S. Million)

Products	Trade of Singapore: Imports of Foods and Raw Materials from S.E. Asia	Trade of Singapore: Exports of Foods and Raw Materials
Coffee, tea, cocoa, spices (07)[a]		68.3
Coffee (071)	22.6	
Spices (075)	41.8	
	64.4	
Crude materials, excl. fuels (2)		420.6
Natural rubber (2311)	332.4	
Wood, Lumber, Cork (24)	38.1	
	370.5	
Mineral fuels (3)		80.0[c]
Petroleum and products	120.0[b]	
Animal, vegetable oils and fats (4)		55.8
Palm oil	37.1	
Coconut oil	10.6	
	47.7	
TOTAL of above categories	602.6	624.7

Source: U.N., *Yearbook of International Trade Statistics, 1973* and *1974*

[a]Standard International Trade Classification categories in parentheses

[b]Estimated value of exports of petroleum to Singapore from Brunei, Sarawak and Indonesia. The principal part of Singapore's petroleum imports during 1970-1972 came from Middle Eastern countries.

[c]Prorated share of Southeast Asian supplies in total exports of petroleum products from Singapore

Table 3

Intraregional Exports of Raw Materials and Foodstuffs In Southeast Asia, 1963-1965

(Annual Average $U.S. Million, Per Cent of Intraregional Exports)

Exporting Country	Live Animals and Food	Beverages and Tobacco	Crude Materials, Inedible	Mineral Fuels, etc.	Animal and Vegetable Oils	Intraregional Exports of Raw Materials	Total Intraregional Exports	Ratio Exports of Raw Materials to Intraregional Exports
	(0)	(1)	(2)	(3)	(4)	(1-4)		(%)
Brunei	-	-	.6	59.6	-	60.2	60.4	99.7
Cambodia	13.4	-	3.3	.1	-	16.8	18.0	93.3
Laos	.1	-	.7	-	-	.8	.7	100.0
Malaysia[1]	41.1	4.1	134.4	40.6	12.0	232.2	284.6	81.6
Singapore	93.7	14.5	20.3	78.6	3.5	210.6	497.5	42.4
Philippines	.3	.1	.4	.4	-	1.2	2.3	52.2
Thailand	128.3	.3	43.8	.7	.1	173.1	175.5	98.6
S. Vietnam	1.5	.2	.7	-	.2	2.6	9.9	26.3
TOTAL	278.3	19.2	204.2	180.0	15.8	697.5	1048.9	66.5

Source: U.N. Economic Commission for Asia and the Far East, Foreign Trade Statistics of Asia and the Far East, 1963, 1964, 1965. Exports classified in Standard International Trade Classification in one digit categories as indicated.

[1] Reported exports of Malaya, Sabah and Sarawak, less mutual trade

SOUTHEAST ASIA'S ECONOMIC DEVELOPMENT IN WORLD PERSPECTIVE

Douglas S. Paauw

I. THE COLONIAL HERITAGE

During the three decades since World War II, Southeast Asian countries have undergone a transition from colonialism. Economic as well as political and social changes have been associated with this process of decolonization. Transition experiences among individual countries has been marked by pronounced variation in economic performance. In some Southeast Asian countries, economic growth and development have proceeded at a pace outstanding in terms of historical growth achievements. In others, economic stagnation has accompanied political and social upheavals stemming from the societies' decolonization struggles.

Prior to World War II, aliens controlled the basic economic decisions in Southeast Asian countries. This external control emphasized the maintenance of a colonial economy, and operated to produce export profits for alien entrepreneurs. Alien profits were based on a pattern of trade in which primary product exports were supplied to the more developed countries in exchange for imports to maintain these aliens and the export sector under their control.

Export profits were the major source of savings in the colonial economy. The economic goal of colonialism was maximizing these profits for transfer abroad. Reinvestment occurred only to expand the size of the export sector during periods of strong world demand for Southeast Asia's primary products. This orientation neglected national development and caused severe fluctuations in investment depending on high prices, prosperity or depressions in the world markets.

Indigenous economic activity consisted of agrarian subsistence production and labor services to the alien-controlled export sector. As population growth occurred and the size of one export sector expanded, population pressure in the indigenous agrarian sector provided growing supplies of cheap labor for employment in export industries. This process exaggerated differences in productivity and income between the indigenous agrarian sector and the export sector. While technological progress occurred in the alien sector of the colonial economy, savings capacity in the indigenous sector was inadequate to improve techniques of production or to raise per capita output. The growing disparities in technology and productivity between the two sectors, a product of colonialism, has come to be known as dualism.

Colonial trade required the development of urban centers and modern transport to accommodate the collection, movement, and processing of primary products for export. Eventually cities developed into modern financial and commercial bases, coordinating the activities of the export sector, as well as serving as the sites of colonial government. Industrial processing of primary products for export, however, occurred near the source of production--primarily on plantations or near mining installations. The development of modern manufacturing industries to serve the domestic market was inconsistent with the goals of colonialism, and manufactured goods were imported, typically from sources in the aliens' home countries. For several centuries, Singapore served as a key center for Southeast Asia's colonial trade, assuming a special entrepôt function because of its strategic location.

The transition from this pervasive colonial system in Southeast Asia to a new growth system was launched by a wave of nationalism and independence after World War II. The common colonial background posed similar transition tasks in these countries. The most basic task was initiating a growth system capable of gradually modernizing the economy on a national scale. The pattern of dualistic colonial growth had to be changed to one in which growth and development forces could permeate the society as a whole. Diversification and development of the nascent industrial base, formerly devoted to export processing, was needed to create an industrial sector serving the entire economy. Integration of this sector with the stagnant, indigenous agrarian sector was a condition for introducing modernizing forces into that backward sector.[1] In welfare terms, the major transition task consisted of raising productivity and employment of domestic labor throughout the economy. This task required that the momentum of export sector growth be harnessed for the economy as a whole.

In Southeast Asia's inherited colonial economies (as in virtually all less-developed countries), there was only one base from which a new growth system could be created. This sole potential source of savings and technology for a national growth system was the colonial export sector. The export surplus, traditionally accruing to aliens who controlled the trade flows, had to be placed under indigenous control and redirected to financing national development. This initial strategy required, however, that the inherited primary product export base be maintained and expanded during transition growth. The success of newly independent countries in

[1] Since Singapore inherited essentially a one-sector urban economy, without an agricultural sector, its transition growth did not involve this fundamental task of modernizing a backward agricultural sector.

Southeast Asia and elsewhere in laying a foundation for a new growth system during the past three decades of transition has been determined primarily by the effectiveness with which this growth base was utilized.

Independence from colonialism (and in the case of Thailand, greater freedom from Western economic domination[2]) was achieved by all Southeast Asian countries by 1960. Immediately after World War II, and in some cases for a considerable period, Southeast Asian countries continued to suffer from the economic dislocations caused by the war. Wartime hostilities and Japanese occupation of these countries had severely crippled the export sectors of these economies. Subsistence output in traditional agriculture had also fallen sharply throughout Southeast Asia.

Rehabilitation of productive capacity to prewar output levels was thus the first major economic challenge facing Southeast Asian countries in the postwar period. Success at this task varied greatly among individual countries, and these differences are significant in explaining subsequent variations in economic performance. Aggregate levels of output were restored to prewar (1938-1939) levels prior to 1950 in Malaya (including Singapore), the Philippines, and Thailand, and by 1950 prewar output per capita had been reachieved in these countries.[3] In Burma and Indonesia, however, where wartime damage to productive capacity was particularly severe and civil strife followed the war, aggregate output was not restored to prewar levels until well into the 1950s. Per capita output in Burma has never recovered to prewar levels, and today per capita output in Indonesia remains near prewar levels. Relative political stability was achieved in Indonesia only in 1966, and significant economic gains have been made since that time. Retrogression continued in Burma throughout the 1960s and into the present decade. Although data are not available for the countries of the Indochina Peninsula (North Vietnam, South Vietnam, Cambodia, and Laos), it may be assumed that the persistence of civil strife throughout the postwar period has prevented significant improvements in their per capita output above prewar levels.

Colonialism left significantly different productive capacities, as measured by per capita output. By the eve of World War II, differences in economic endowments

---

[2]Though Thailand had never been a colony in the formal political sense, her economy was clearly of the colonial type prior to World War II.

[3]This and other assertions in this section are based on data in Douglas S. Paauw, "Economic Progress in Southeast Asia," Journal of Asian Studies 23 (November 1963): 69-92.

and variations in colonial policy were reflected in growing disparities in the structures and performance of Southeast Asian economies. To provide a rough estimate of the resulting differences in productive capacity, we need a common unit of measurement. We follow convention by using per capita gross domestic product in United States dollars. Table 1 presents this measure for Southeast Asian countries for 1950, 1960, and 1970. The U.S. dollar estimates of per capita gross domestic product for 1950 are a rough index of productivity levels inherited from colonialism, qualified, of course, by different rates of recovery from the economic losses sustained during World War II.

In 1950, Malaysia (U.S. $189) and Singapore (U.S. $247) ranked substantially above the other countries--with per capita output levels more than double the value of the third ranked country, the Philippines (U.S. $95). The other countries, all with per capita product levels below U.S. $85, showed significant disparity: Vietnam, U.S. $84; Thailand, U.S. $62; Indonesia, U.S. $50; and Burma, U.S. $44. It is interesting to observe that the 1950s' rankings were maintained in 1960, and that in 1970 the only change was Thailand's forging ahead of the Republic of Vietnam.[4]

The preeminence of output per capita in West Malaysia (then known as Malaya) and Singapore confirms a particularly favorable heritage left by colonialism. The population and natural resource endowments in Malaya (then including Singapore) encouraged the British to create a large colonial enclave, devoted to production and processing of valuable land-based primary products, especially rubber and tin. In view of the small indigenous population relative to natural resources, labor for these enclave activities was attracted from populous Asian countries, particularly from China and India. At the time (1957) of Malaya's independence, three-fourths of the labor force was employed in the export enclave.[5] This contrasts with much smaller enclave employment of labor in other Southeast Asian countries at the time of decolonization--averaging under one-fourth of the employed labor force.

This dominance of economic activity by the export enclave explains the superior

---

[4]Changes between 1950, 1960, and 1970 are not indicative of growth of real product per capita since the estimates are in current U.S. dollars, reflecting dollar purchasing power in the years cited.

[5]Douglas S. Paauw and John C.H. Fei, The Transition in Open Dualistic Economies: Theory and Southeast Asian Experience (New Haven: Yale University Press, 1973), pp. 207-208.

Table 1

Per Capita Gross Domestic Product[6]
(In U.S. Dollars of Current Purchasing Power)

Country	1950	1960	1970
Burma	44	61	78
Indonesia	50	77	107
Malaysia, West	189	278	313
Philippines	95	165	255
Singapore	247	431	916
Thailand	62	96	180
Vietnam, Republic	84	108	123

[6] Derived from the following sources, with adjustments for current U.S. dollar purchasing power:

United Nations, Department of Economic and Social Affairs, *Yearbook of National Accounts Statistics*, (ST/ESA/STAT/SER. 0/4), 1974 and various issues (Republic of Vietnam estimate for 1968 adjusted to reflect growth of real product and purchasing power changes).

Also for 1950, United Nations, Department of Economic and Social Affairs, Economic Commission for Asia and the Far East, *Economic Survey of Asia and the Far East*, (E/CN. 11/ECON. SUR.), various issues.

Paauw, "Economic Progress . . .," (fn. 3), pp. 69-92.

levels of per capita product inherited from colonialism by West Malaysia[7] and Singapore. Labor productivity in export activities was several times as great as in traditional agriculture throughout Southeast Asia. In simple terms, a much larger share of the population participated in the fruits of the enclave's superior technology in Malaysia and Singapore than elsewhere in Southeast Asia. As an urban state, Singapore possessed the additional advantage of not inheriting from colonialism a large agricultural sector, a sector whose low productivity, high population pressure, and backward technology have presented the major drag on general economic progress.

Another striking feature of the colonial heritage in Southeast Asia was the degree to which these economies were linked to the world market at the time of independence. Growth and development of the export sector were the focus of alien entrepreneurs in the colonial enclave, and this focus engendered a high level of primary product exports from the land resources of these countries. Earnings from these exports were used to provide imports to maintain and expand the export sector and to finance profit transfers abroad.

The export orientation of Southeast Asian countries under colonialism, just prior to independence, can be measured by the ratio of exports to aggregate product. Data in Table 2 show that this ratio varied from 46 percent in Malaya (including Singapore) to 19 percent in Thailand. Except for Malaya, the export ratios shown are typical of those found for colonial countries. Malaya's unusually high export ratio reflects the high degree of export-oriented economic activity mentioned above.

From the viewpoint of post-independence development, the large export sector in Southeast Asian countries offered an important link to world market sources of capital and technological inputs, required for diversification of growth. Hence, maintenance and expansion of primary product exports, combined with redirection of export earnings to finance national development, were essential for successfully launching a transition from colonial economies to growth for national development. Export performance is, therefore, the first and most important indicator of Southeast Asia's growth prospects after independence.

---

[7] Henceforth, the term Malaysia will be used and will consistently refer to West Malaysia, except where noted.

Table 2

Ratio of Exports to Aggregate Product[8]

Country	1938	1958-60[9]
Burma	33	17
Indonesia	24	13
Malaya	46[10]	47
Philippines	20	18
Thailand	19	17

[8] Paauw, "Economic Progress . . .," (fn. 3), Table 6, p. 80, updated by data from UN, Yearbook . . . (fn. 6).

[9] Average for 1958, 1959, and 1960.

[10] Average, 1947-49, Malaya including Singapore.

II. EXPORTS AND GROWTH

Transition growth in Southeast Asian economies began from the colonial heritage just described. In a fundamental sense, the transition from a colonial export economy to more diversified growth for indigenous welfare requires effective utilization of the primary product export base. The initial size of this growth base and its expansion are important determinants of progress toward a new growth system.

The relationship between growth of per capita real product and the volume of exports is shown in Table 3 for five Southeast Asian Countries for which data are available.[11] Disregarding for the moment the relative size of the export sector, these data nevertheless show that the maintenance and expansion of the colonial economy's export volume were essential to launch growth of per capita real product after 1950.

Two countries, Burma and Indonesia, showed almost persistent stagnation of per capita real product between 1937 and 1970. In Burma, export volumes never approached the pre-independence (1937) level, although the export volume rose during the 1950s from 34 per cent of prewar to 47 per cent in 1960. This failure to restore the colonial export volume was accompanied by per capita real product remaining below the prewar level throughout the period 1950-1970. During the 1950s, per capita real product rose from 57 per cent of prewar to 84 per cent,[12] but stagnated at the latter level during the 1960s as export volume fell.

Indonesia's export volume and per capita product both showed fluctuations near stagnant levels from 1950 to 1965. During this period, export volume rose by only 8 per cent and per capita real product by 12 per cent, with per capita real product in 1965 still at the 1937 level. Since 1965, the growth performance of the Indonesian economy has shown dramatic improvement. Export volume grew by 33 per cent between 1965 and 1970 and by 79 per cent in the brief four year period, 1970-1974.[13]

---

[11] More detailed data on export volume and growth of real product are presented in Appendix A, Tables A-1 and A-2, respectively.

[12] A reasonable explanation of this progress in the 1950s is that growth continued to consist of rehabilitation from World War II economic retrogression. In other Southeast Asian countries, restoration of per capita output levels to prewar benchmarks after World War II was accompanied by very high growth rates of per capita real product, in some cases exceeding 10 per cent.

[13] 1970-1974 data from International Monetary Fund, International Financial Statistics (Published jointly by the International Monetary Fund and the International Bank for Reconstruction and Development), February, 1976.

Table 3

Indexes of Real Product Per Capita and Export Volume
1937-1970 (1937 = 100)[14]

Year	Burma		Indonesia		Malaysia		Philippines		Thailand	
	Per Cap. Real Prod.	Export Volume	Per Cap. Real Prod.	Export Volume	Per Cap. Real Prod.	Export Volume	Per Cap. Real Prod.	Export Volume	Per Cap. Real Prod.	Export Volume
1937	100	100	100	100	100	100	100	100	100	100
1950	57	34	90	118	141	153	100	109	142	143
1960	84	47	105	112	141	167	131	162	171	149
1965	--	--	101	128	--	--	--	--	--	--
1970	85	22	109	170	195	268	161	235	279	228

[14] Real Product Per Capita: 1950-1970: See Appendix A, Table A-2.

1937-1950: Paauw, "Economic Progress . . .," (fn. 3).

Export Volume: See Appendix A, Table A-1.

After falling during the first half of the 1960 decade, per capita real product rose by 11 per cent in the second half; and by an additional 13 per cent from 1970 to 1973. The Indonesian economy, therefore, failed to initiate transition growth during the 1950-1965 period, but exhibited a sharp turnaround toward new growth momentum after 1965. It is quite clear that this escape from a decade and a half of stagnation was associated with a sudden upsurge of exports after domestic political stability was established in late 1965.

The three other countries for which 1950-1970 data are available (Malaysia, the Philippines, and Thailand) showed significant but erratic progress in raising both export volume and per capita real product above prewar levels. The Philippines barely restored prewar levels by 1950, but enjoyed rapid progress during the 1950s, raising export volume by 49 per cent and per capita real product by 31 per cent. In Malaysia and Thailand, however, the 1950s was a decade of modest performance. Although export volume grew by only 4 per cent in Thailand, per capita real product was raised by 20 per cent. Malaysia failed to raise per capita real product, and export volume grew by only 9 per cent. It should be borne in mind that Malaysia (then Malaya) suffered from domestic insurrections and achieved independence only near the end of the 1950s.

During the 1960s, rapid transition growth was finally launched in Malaysia and Thailand, while progress in the Philippines continued, but at a slackening pace. During that decade, real product per capita was raised by 63 per cent in Thailand, accompanied by a 53 per cent increase in exports volume. In Malaysia, export volume grew by 60 per cent, but real product per capita was raised by a much smaller percentage--38 per cent. In the Philippines, the growth of export volume (45 per cent) was also more rapid than growth of real product per capita (23 per cent).

Per Capita Exports and Import Capacity

In view of the fundamental growth contribution of exports in providing import capacity for industrialization and modernization of agriculture, a scale factor is needed to assess the relative magnitude of this contribution in different countries. In the ultimate sense, growth and development must be evaluated on a per capita basis since labor requires capital, modern inputs, and improved technology to raise its productivity in all sectors. This viewpoint suggests that measurement of exports *per capita* is more appropriate than mere aggregative comparisons.

To provide a common basis for comparison, export earnings per capita are presented in current United States dollars. These data are presented for 1950, 1960, and 1970 in Table 4.[15] The 1950 data are useful as a scale factor to assess the relative size of the export sector left by colonialism near the beginning of transition growth. The earlier observation that the size of the colonial export sector was much larger in Malaysia than elsewhere is borne out; Malaysia's U.S. dollar export earnings in 1950 were 14 times as large as the average for the other four countries (Burma, Indonesia, the Philippines, and Thailand). This is a fundamental explanation for the large differences in 1950 per capita GDP given in Table 1 (U.S. $189 for Malaysia compared to an average of U.S. $63 for the other countries). These sharp differences in per capita export capacity inherited from colonialism are important in explaining subsequent growth performance.

The slow-growth countries, Burma and Indonesia, not only began with per capita export capacity substantially below those of other Southeast Asian countries, but this capacity fell over the 1950-1970 period (by 58 per cent in Burma and 10 per cent in Indonesia). In the other countries, where substantial growth progress was made, per capita export capacity was increased over that period. It should be observed, however, that the change in per capita exports was rather closely related to variations in growth performance between the 1950 and the 1960 decade. For example, Malaysia's per capita exports fell by 15 per cent over the 1950s and per capita real product showed no gain. During the 1960s, Malaysia's high level of per capita exports rose by 11 per cent and per capital real product grew at an annual rate of 3.3 per cent. Similar relationships existed in Thailand where growth of per capita exports in the 1950s rose from the 1950s rate of 3 per cent to 21 per cent, and the average annual rate of growth or real product per capita rose from 1.9 to 5 per cent.[16] In the Philippines, per capita export capacity rose more rapidly in the 1960s than in the 1950s, but the per capita real product growth rate receded somewhat (from 2.7 to 2.1) in the 1960s.

Singapore's per capita export earnings are shown for 1960 and 1970. Singapore's per capita exports of $661 and $719 for the beginning and end of the 1960 decade are overwhelming when compared to the other countries. This exceedingly high level of per capita exports was not only maintained but expanded over the decade. Singapore's capacity to preserve this favorable colonial heritage, together

---

[15] To avoid distortion from an erratic initial or terminal year, three year averages of U.S. dollar export earnings are used for 1960 and 1970.

[16] Per capita real product growth rates by periods are presented in Appendix A, Table A-2.

Table 4

Export Earnings Per Capita[17,18]
(In U.S. Dollars of Current Purchasing Power)

Country	1950	1960	1970	Percentage Change 1950-1960	Percentage Change 1960-1970
Burma	7.5	10.4	4.4	+ 39	- 58
Indonesia	10.5	8.1	7.3	- 23	- 10
Malaysia	178.4	155.0	172.0	- 13	+ 11
Philippines	16.3	19.0	25.8	+ 17	+ 36
Singapore	--	661.0	719.0	--	+ 9
Thailand	16.0	16.5	19.9	+ 3	+ 21

[17] 1960 and 1970 figures are three-year averages.

[18] Exports and Exchange Rates, 1950: United Nations, Secretariat, Statistical Office, International Trade Statistics, (ST/STAT/SER. M/52).

Exports in U.S. dollars, 1960 and 1970: Burma, Singapore, and Thailand; United Nations, Department of Economic and Social Affairs, Economic Commission for Asia and the Far East, Statistical Yearbook, (ST/ESA/STAT/SER. S/2). Indonesia, Malaysia, and Philippines; IMF, International Financial Statistics, (fn. 13).

Population: United Nations, Department of Economic and Social Affairs, Demographic Yearbook, (ST/ESA/STAT/R/3).

with the absence of a backward agricultural sector, go far toward explaining Singapore's uniquely superior growth performance during the 1960 decade. Singapore's growth experience suggests that rapid expansion of exports is not needed for superior growth performance if a high level of per capita exports can be maintained and the import capacity effectively utilized. To a somewhat lesser extent, this argument also applies to Malaysia, where per capita exports were raised modestly (by 11 per cent) from $155 to $172 over the decade.

The corollary of this argument is that where per capita levels of exports inherited from colonialism were modest, as in the other Southeast Asian countries, substantial progress in raising per capita exports are a precondition for satisfactory transition growth performance. This precondition was achieved in the Philippines and Thailand, and the variations between export performance and growth achievements in these countries must be explained on other grounds. We shall see in the final section that differences in growth strategies offer a partial explanation. The data for Burma and Indonesia suggest that falling per capita levels of exports are, indeed, a concomitant of economic stagnation.

The differences between per capita export capacity and growth performance in Southeast Asian countries are, in some cases, partly explained by the additional import capacity provided by foreign capital inflows. Table 5 presents data (1950, 1960, and 1970) on total import capacity per capita by adding per capita capital inflows to per capita exports, both components being measured in United States dollars of current purchasing power.[19]

The estimates of per capita capital inflows for 1950 reveal that foreign capital inflows played a minor role in Southeast Asian growth at the start of the transition from colonialism. At the beginning of the 1950 decade foreign capital flows were positive only for Indonesia (accounting for 22 per cent of per capita import capacity of $13.4) and the Philippines (2 per cent of per capita import capacity of $16.61). In Burma, Malaysia and Thailand, foreign capital flowed outward in the early 1950s, and in fact, throughout much of the 1950 decade. This phenomenon should be viewed as a continuation of the colonial tradition of foreign profit transfers from the primary product export sector. This remnant of colonialism

---

[19]Foreign capital inflow estimates are of the national income accounting type, representing the difference between total foreign expenditures on domestic goods and services, and total domestic expenditures on foreign goods and services. Estimates in Table 5 are three-year averages since such capital flows may show erratic behavior in particular years.

Table 5

Per Capita Import Capacity, 1950, 1960 and 1970[20,21]
(In U.S. Dollars of Current Purchasing Power)

Country	1950			1960			1970			Percentage Change 1950-60			Percentage Change 1960-70		
	Exports	Capital Inflow	Total	Exports	Capital Inflow	Total	Exports	Capital Inflow	Total	Exports	Capital Inflow	Total	Exports	Capital Inflow	Total
Burma	7.5	-2.8	4.7	10.4	.7	11.1	4.4	1.2	5.6	+39	--	+136	-58	+ 71	- 50
Indonesia	10.5	2.9	13.4	8.1	.9	10.0	7.3	4.1	11.4	-23	-69	-25	-10	+355	+ 14
Malaysia	178.4	-65.8	112.6	155.0	-21.6	133.4	172.0	-20.7	151.3	-13	--	+18	+11	--	+ 13
Philippines	16.3	.3	16.6	19.0	4.3	23.3	25.8	6.1	31.9	+17	+1333	+40	+36	+ 42	+ 80
Singapore	--	--	--	661.0	55.0	716.0	719.0	173.9	892.9	--	--	--	+ 9	+216	+125
Thailand	16.0	-2.1	13.9	16.5	.9	17.4	19.9	7.6	27.5	+3	--	+25	+21	+777	+ 58

[20] Three-year averages.

[21] Per Capita Exports: Table 4.

Per Capita Capital Inflow:

1950: UN, ECAFE, Economic Survey . . . (fn. 6), various issues, (Exchange Rates from IMF, International Financial Statistics, (fn. 13).

1960 and 1970: UN, Yearbook . . . (fn. 6); Population from UN, Demographic Yearbook, (fn. 18); Exchange rates from IMF, International Financial Statistics, (fn. 13).

persisted in Malaysia, where per capita capital outflows remained large throughout the 1950-1970 period.

Excepting Malaysia, capital inflows turned positive for the five other countries by 1960, but contributed significantly to per capita import capacity only in the Philippines (18 per cent of per capita import capacity). This contribution helps to explain the Philippines' expansion of per capita real product during the 1950s (2.7 per cent per year) while exports per capita were not growing at an impressive rate (17 per cent over the decade, or 1.6 per cent per year). Positive capital inflow had contributed 60 per cent of the rise in per capita import capacity over the 1950 decade, permitting that capacity to rise by 40 per cent (3.4 per cent per year).

During the 1960 decade, per capita capital inflows again rose for all countries except Malaysia, where capital outflows continued at approximately the same level as during the 1950s. By the end of the 1960 decade, these inflows were contributing substantially to per capita import capacity in all the other countries (Burma, 21 per cent; Indonesia, 36 per cent; Philippines, 19 per cent; Singapore, 24 per cent; and Thailand, 28 per cent). Nevertheless, during the 1960 decade, per capita import capacity in Burma (U.S. $ 5.6 in 1970) was inadequate to raise per capita real product. In Indonesia, where improvement in per capita import capacity from both exports and foreign capital outflow recurred only after 1965 and reached U.S. $ 11.4 by 1970, per capita real product remained almost stagnant during the 1960s (rising only 4.1 per cent or .4 per cent per year).

In the Philippines, the increasing contribution of foreign capital failed to prevent the annual growth of real product per capita from falling from the annual average of 2.7 per cent during the 1950s to 2.1 per cent during the 1960s. In Thailand, where impressive gains were made in raising the average per capita real product growth rate from 1.9 per cent to 5.0 per cent, foreign capital inflows undoubtedly played a significant role. Exports raised per capita import capacity by 21 per cent and (from $ 16.5 to $ 19.9) between 1960 and 1970 while foreign capital inflows caused total import capacity per capita to rise by 58 per cent (from $ 17.4 to $ 27.5).

The data in Table 5 reflect two unique situations, Malaysia and Singapore. Unlike other countries, Malaysia's capital outflow, equivalent to over 40 per cent of her gross capital formation, once again emphasizes her favorable colonial heritage. The relatively high levels of per capita output and exports enabled Malaysia to entirely finance a domestic capital formation (about 15 per cent of GDP) as well as to transfer a large volume of per capita savings abroad. Singapore's case is opposite in nature. Extremely high levels of capital inflow throughout the 1960 decade permitted that country to substantially raise the domestic capital formation rate. Massive per capita capital inflows must certainly be included among the basic explanations of Singapore's outstanding growth performance during the 1960 decade.

III. COMPONENTS OF GROWTH

In this section, the focus shifts to domestic aspects of growth in Southeast Asian economies during the two decades of transition, 1950-1970. These aspects reflect the effectiveness with which import capacity was utilized to initiate new systems for diversification of growth beyond the confines of the export sectors inherited from colonialism. This survey of the domestic components of growth provides background for the interpretations of growth performance offered in the next section.

Capital Formation

Capital formation plays a vital role in the growth and diversification of industry as well as in the modernization of agriculture during the transition. While exports and foreign capital inflow provide foreign exchange resources and may enhance saving potential, they must be converted into capital formation if the labor force is to be equipped with modern producer goods. For this reason, capital formation rates are an important general index of the development status of economies in transition.

In Table 6, capital formation data are presented for two periods, 1960-62 and 1968-70.[22] Gross capital formation rates, shown in the first three columns, are a general comparative measure of developmental effort among countries. Except for the stagnant economy of Burma (where the gross capital formation rate fell by 59 per cent over the 1960 decade, from 17 to 7 per cent), capital formation rates were raised. Indonesia's gain of 50 per cent to a modest rate of 12 per cent was achieved in the 1965-70 period. Singapore's exceptionally large gain in her gross

---

[22] All data on capital formation rates are three-year averages near the beginning and end of the 1960 decade. Data represent ratios of gross capital formation (including changes in stocks) to gross domestic product. Singapore data, however, refer to gross fixed capital formation only.

Table 6

Capital Formation Indicators[23]

Country	Gross Capital Formation Rates			Capital Formation Per Capita (U.S. Dollars)		
	1960-62	1968-70	Percentage Change	1960-62	1968-70	Percentage Change
Burma[24]	17	7	-59	11	7	-36
Indonesia	8	12	50	6	11	83
Malaysia, West	14	15	7	46	49	7
Philippines	17	20	18	27	45	67
Singapore[25]	9	19	111	46	163	254
Thailand	17	25	47	18	44	144

[23] Capital formation and Foreign Capital Inflow: UN, Yearbook . . . (fn. 6).

Population: UN, Demographic Yearbook, (fn. 18).

Exchange Rates: IMF, International Financial Statistics, (fn. 13).

[24] All data, 1960-62 and 1966-68.

[25] Singapore gross capital formation data are fixed capital formation only, excluding stocks; all data 1961-63 and 1968-70.

fixed capital formation rate[26] (111 per cent, from 9 to 19 per cent) is consistent with her outstanding growth performance. Thailand's capacity to raise the capital formation rate during the 1960 decade by 47 per cent to Southeast Asia's highest rate (25 per cent) is consistent with sharp acceleration of per capita real product growth from an annual average of 1.9 per cent in the 1950s to 5.0 per cent in the 1960s. Modest gains were recorded in Malaysia (+7 per cent) and the Philippines (+18 per cent). If the capital formation data are accurate, Malaysia was able to achieve a somewhat higher per capita product growth rate than the Philippines with a lower gross capital formation rate. This might be interpreted to indicate more efficient use of capital stock in Malaysia than the Philippines.

Since successful transition involves equipping the population as a whole with more modern means of production, per capita capital formation data are helpful in understanding transition progress. Estimates of gross capital formation per capita, in United States dollars of current purchasing power, are also found in Table 6. These estimates furnish an additional dimension of the diversity of Southeast Asia's growth performance during the 1960 decade. Once again, Singapore's performance excels, as that country raised per capita capital formation from $46 to $163, an increase of 254 per cent. By the end of the decade, per capita capital formation in Malaysia, the Philippines, and Thailand was at approximately the same level (between $45 and $50). Thailand's performance in raising per capita capital formation by 144 per cent to this level is further confirmation of her unusual growth achievements over the decade. The low levels of per capita capital formation in Burma and Indonesia are consistent with the 1960 decade's record of stagnation in those countries. We note, however, that Indonesia made significant progress in raising the level (entirely during the second half of the decade), while Burma's per capital formation fell sharply.

Structural Change

Structural change, in which output and factor employment shift from agriculture to industry, is a necessary feature of a successful transition.[27] These shifts

---

[26] As noted in the accompanying table, capital formation data for Singapore refer only to gross *fixed* capital formation, excluding changes in stocks.

[27] See, for example, Hollis B. Chenery, "Patterns of Industrial Growth," *American Economic Review*, Vol. 50 (September 1960): 624-54, and Simon Kuznets, *Economic Growth and Structure* (New York: W. W. Norton & Company, Inc., 1965).

occur as manufacturing and its supporting activities in the industrial sector evolve from their function of servicing primary product exports to perform more diversified growth functions. Table 7 presents estimates of the percentage shares of manufacturing and of the entire industrial sector in aggregate product for three periods: 1950-52, 1958-60, and 1968-70.

The 1950 Decade

These data indicate that only one country--the Philippines--showed substantial progress in raising the shares of both manufacturing and the broader industrial sector during the 1950 decade. Rapid expansion of the manufacturing sector (from 9.3 to 17.3 per cent of aggregate product) was accompanied by general industrial growth, as the entire industrial sector grew from 17.8 to 25.8 per cent of aggregate product. This performance, unique in Southeast Asia, reflects the successful pursuit of an import substitution strategy in the Philippines. The Philippine economy was effectively shaped by powerful policy forces to channel export earnings into investment for import-replacement manufacturing industries.[28] This impetus in manufacturing created strong inducements for expansion of the other components of the industrial sector in, for example, construction, power, and transport.

Changes in manufacturing and industrial shares in the other countries during the 1950 decade require careful analysis. To assist in analyzing these changes, the percentage changes in the shares of both manufacturing and industry are also shown in Table 7.

Indonesia stands out as the country showing least progress in structural change during the 1950 decade; manufacturing's share in aggregate product fell by 7.5 per cent over the 1950 decade while the share of industry rose by only 5.4 per cent. This confirms the earlier finding that Indonesia's economy was essentially stagnant. Similar to the Philippines, Indonesia aggressively pursued an import substitution strategy during the 1950 decade. In the Indonesian case, however, the strategy failed. Import-replacement industries grew too slowly to spark growth in either the industrial sector or the economy as a whole. The reasons behind this failure in Indonesia are too complex to examine here. We have noted, however, that one basic cause lay in stagnation of exports since export earnings are the major source to finance the heavy requirements of capital goods imports for investment in manufacturing industries.

---

[28] Paauw and Fei, The Transition . . . (fn. 6), Chapter 7.

Table 7

Manufacturing and Industrial[29] Sectors As Percentage of Aggregate Product, 1950, 1960, and 1970[30]

	1950-52 (average)		1958-60 (average)		1968-70 (average)		Percentage Changes			
							1950-52 to 1958-60		1958-60 to 1968-70	
Country	Mfg.	Industry	Mfg.	Industry	Mfg.	Industry	Mfg.	Industry	Mfg.	Industry
Burma	10.2	16.4	12.5	21.3	9.4[32]	19.3[32]	+22.5	+29.8	-24.8	- 9.4
Indonesia	8.5[31]	14.8[31]	7.9	15.6	9.0	19.6	- 7.5	+ 5.4	13.9	25.6
Malaysia	5.6	16.1	7.8	17.0	11.9	22.0	+39.2	+ 5.6	52.6	29.4
Philippines	9.3	17.8	17.3	25.8	15.2	22.4	+86.0	+35.9	-12.1	-15.5
Singapore	--	--	9.0	NA	17.3	NA	--	--	92.2	NA
Thailand	11.9	18.4	11.3	25.0	16.1	31.3	- 5.3	+35.9	42.5	25.2

[29] Industry, as a broader concept than manufacturing, is defined to include mining, manufacturing, construction, utilities (electricity, gas and water) and transport, storage, and communication. In this sense, industry is similar to Kuznets M+ sector. (See Simon Kuznets, "Quantitative Aspects of Economic Growth of Nations II: Industrial Distribution of National Product and Labor Force," Economic Development and Cultural Change, Supplement to Volume V, July 1957, p. 54.)

[30] For all countries except West Malaysia: UN, Yearbook . . . (fn. 6).

For West Malaysia: V. V. Bhanoji Rao, The Postwar Development Pattern and Policy of the Malaysian Economy, University of Singapore, Ph.D. Dissertation, March 1974, Table C2, p. 368.

[31] 1951 and 1952 average.

[32] 1965 and 1967 average.

In Burma, structural change during the 1950s ranked second in Southeast Asia as the share of manufacturing grew by 22.5 per cent and industry by 29.8 per cent. However, this progress occurred under a development strategy which placed excessive emphasis on rapidly creating a capital-intensive industrial sector. Rehabilitation of agriculture and primary product exports, from the severe retrogressions which occurred during the previous decade, were neglected.[33] Subsequent experience in Burma has demonstrated that this strategy of isolating one growth sector from the economy is doomed to failure.

Unlike Burma, Indonesia, and the Philippines, the other two countries--Malaysia and Thailand--did not pursue aggressive industrialization strategies during the 1950s.[34] In Malaysia, the 1950s were devoted to agricultural diversification and to strengthening the economy's capacity to maintain and expand its primary product exports which required a heavy input of industrial processing. The share of the industrial sector in aggregate product there rose modestly by 5.6 per cent, while the impressive growth in manufacturing (+39.2 per cent) was associated with primary product export processing rather than import substitution for the domestic market.[35]

In Thailand, an alternative strategy for primary product export expansion was pursued, emphasizing diversification of the traditionally unprocessed Thai exports, through introduction of new export crops. This strategy required large-scale investment in transport, irrigation, and construction to open up new agricultural areas to cultivation and to provide access to markets. In this type of growth milieu, manufacturing was neglected while those components of industrial sector growth (transport, for example) needed for export product diversification were actively promoted. As a result, the share of the broad industrial sector in aggregate product grew by 35.9 per cent during the 1950s, while the share of manufacturing fell (by 5.3 per cent). The payoff from this strategy, in terms of rapid growth of exports and an accelerating rate of growth of real product, however, did not occur until the 1960s.

---

[33]Paauw, "Economic Progress . . .," (fn. 3), pp. 88-89.

[34]In Thailand, an import substitution strategy was pursued during the early 1950s but was abandoned when it was recognized to have failed.

[35]In 1960, the first Malaysian interindustry account indicated that the export sector absorbed 70 per cent of manufacturing's output. Malaya, Department of Statistics, Interindustry Account, 1960 (Kuala Lumpur: no date).

This analysis of the relationship between structural change and primary product export expansion explains why manufactured exports were not introduced in Southeast Asia during the initial transition phase of the 1950s. To sum up, Burma and Indonesia neglected export expansion while concentrating on import substitution. This industrialization strategy failed, however, and a viable manufacturing sector was not created in either country. In the Philippines, an import substitution strategy was effective in creating a substantial manufacturing sector through reliance on transferring the growing primary product export earnings to industrial entrepreneurs.[36] The very success of this strategy, however, required an incentive system which discouraged manufactured exports.[37] In Malaysia and in Thailand, development strategy accorded highest priority to primary product export expansion and land resources were available to insure success. Manufacturing and industrial sector growth was linked to primary product export development as industry provided intermediate goods and services to the export sector. Consumer goods manufactures to replace imports lagged, offering no basis for shifting from primary product to manufactured exports.

The 1960 Decade

We have seen that the Philippines outpaced other Southeast Asian countries in accomplishing structural change during the 1950s. During the 1960s, however, the emergence of new growth strategies elsewhere and the exhaustion of import substitution growth in the Philippines led to very different records of structural change among the transitional economies in Southeast Asia.

In Burma, the retrogression in structural change (manufacturing, -24.8 per cent; industry, -9.4 per cent) was consistent with our general finding of overall stagnation. In Indonesia, however, positive structural change occurred in both manufacturing's share (13.9 per cent increase) and industry's share (25.6 per cent increase). This progress was made entirely between 1965 and 1970, the period during which the new regime reversed the long course toward stagnation. While manufacturing's share was essentially restored to the level of the early 1950s, the share of industry was raised well above any level previously achieved. This

---

[36] For a detailed analysis of this profit transfer mechanism under an import substitution growth regime, see Paauw and Fei, <u>The Transition</u> . . ., (fn. 5), Chapters 3 and 7.

[37] <u>Ibid</u>., Chapter 7.

divergence between expanding the share of manufacturing and that of the broader industrial sector is indicative not only of the absence of an aggressive import substitution strategy in the policies of the post-1965 regime, but also of the emphasis placed upon reviving the industrial infrastructure to accommodate recovery of Indonesia's traditionally diversified primary product exports.

Agricultural and Industrial Growth

Both industrialization and modernization of agriculture are needed for a successful transition from a colonial-type primary product export economy to a more diversified growth system. In the context of inherited dualism, progress toward modern growth necessarily involves integration of industry and traditional agriculture. Industrial growth momentum cannot be maintained (as we have seen from Burma's experience) if the agricultural sector remains stagnant. This is true because the relationship between growth of agriculture and industry is symbiotic in nature. Industrial sector growth requires access to growing domestic supplies of food and raw materials as well as the release of labor from agriculture for industrial employment. In addition, agriculture remains basic (excepting the petroleum export economy of Indonesia) as the source of primary product exports, which still dominate in financing the import components of industrial growth.

Since industrial sector growth must spark change in the traditional agricultural sector, import capacity created by primary product exports must be utilized to provide capital, technology, and intermediate goods to feed industrial development. Diffusion of growth momentum throughout the economy as a whole depends on the capacity of industry to strengthen supply and demand relationships with the agricultural sector.

Data showing average annual rates of growth of agriculture and manufacturing during the 1960s are presented in Table 8.[38] Singapore's exceptionally high manufacturing growth rate (14.5 per cent) is indicative of manufacturing's role as the leading growth sector, both domestically and in exports, in an economy free from the drag of a backward traditional agricultural sector. Manufacturing's impressive growth rates in Thailand (11.1 per cent) and Malaysia (10.2 per cent) during the 1960s were accompanied by relatively high rates of growth of agricultural output, 5.5 per cent and 6.0 per cent, respectively. In both

---

[38]All growth rates referred to in this paragraph are average annual rates.

Table 8

Growth of Agriculture and Manufacturing, 1960-1970[39]
(Average Annual Growth Rates of Value Added, Constant Prices)

Country	Agriculture	Manufacturing
Burma[40]	2.8	3.3
Indonesia	2.1	3.3
Malaysia	6.0	10.2
Philippines	4.0	5.8
Singapore	---	14.5
Thailand	5.5	11.1

[39] UN, Yearbook . . . (fn. 6), 1974, except Malaysia.
Malaysia: V. V. Bhanoji Rao, National Accounts of West Malaysia, 1947-1971 (Singapore: Hinemann Educational Books Ltd., 1976).

[40] 1962-1970.

countries, the acceleration of industrial growth during the 1960s reflected a shift toward emphasis on industrialization for the domestic market. Import substitution began to occur, tempered by continued close linkage between manufacturing and primary production (both exports and traditional agriculture). Modest growth of manufacturing output in the Philippines (5.8 per cent per year) continued to outpace expansion of agricultural output (4.0 per cent per year), even though a shift in national policy occurred in the middle of the decade, giving higher priority to agricultural development. In the stagnant economy of Burma, annual growth of both manufacturing (3.3 per cent) and agricultural output (2.8 per cent) barely kept ahead of population growth (2.2 per cent per year). In Indonesia, both manufacturing and agriculture grew slowly during the 1960s (with annual growth rates for manufacturing of 2.9 per cent and for agriculture of 2.3 per cent), but performance in the second half of the decade was substantially better than in the first half.

The agricultural sector's transition growth role is dual in nature; this sector must provide food and raw materials for the domestic economy as well as export earnings to accommodate import-dependent growth of the industrial sector during the first several decades of transition growth. In the stagnant economies of Burma and Indonesia, the agricultural sector remained sluggish in both roles during the entire 1950-1970 period. In Malaysia, the Philippines, and Thailand, however, export agriculture showed considerably better performance than the good-producing sector.[41]

Long-run productivity indexes for non-export agriculture are available only for Indonesia, the Philippines, and Thailand. Bairoch's estimates for these countries cover the prewar period to 1968-1972, and refer to productivity per male laborer in food-producing agriculture in terms of the average annual production of millions of net direct calories.[42] Bairoch's results show relatively stagnant productivity in all three countries but with Thailand's absolute productivity substantially above Indonesia and the Philippines--consistent with Thailand's superior land-population ratio. Bairoch's estimates are as follows:

---

[41] For Malaysia, this statement is supported by data from Rao, _National Accounts_ . . . (fn. 39), especially Chapter 5. For the Philippines and Thailand the evidence is contained in Paul Bairoch, _The Economic Development of the Third World Since 1900_ (London: Methuen & Co., Ltd., 1975).

[42] _Ibid._, _The Economic Development_ . . . , pp. 22-39. Net refers to productivity corrected for seed used.

	24 LDC's	Indonesia	Philippines	Thailand
1934-38	5.3	3.7	4.7	6.2
1946-50	5.0	3.7	4.5	6.5
1953-57	5.7	4.7	5.1	6.7
1960-64	5.6	4.6	4.8	6.8
1968-70	5.5	4.5	4.6	7.2

Thus, the inherited colonial bias against traditional agricultural development persisted throughout the first generation of transition growth. Emphasis continued upon primary product exports, while the major change from colonialism was a shift in growth priorities toward the industrial sector. A key question in future Southeast Asian development, therefore, is whether or not the manufacturing sector will be capable of transmitting growth to the traditional agricultural sector.

Per Capita Manufactures

Assessment of the capacity of manufacturing to generate economy-wide growth momentum should be considered on a per capita basis. For this purpose, Table 9 presents estimates of per capita manufacturing value added (in current U.S. dollars) at the beginning and end of the 1960 decade, and the change in these values over the decade. The commanding position of Singapore, where per capita manufactures rose from $41.4 to $145.0 over the decade, must be understood in the context of Singapore's single-sector, urban economy. The growth of per capita manufactures at a decade rate of 250 per cent (9.6 per cent per year) was a major component in Singapore's exceptionally high growth rate of per capita GDP (7.2 per cent). The manufacturing sector stimulated growth throughout the single industrial sector economy, while earnings from the high level of per capita exports provided capital and raw materials as well as domestic demand for rapid industrial expansion.

Substantial progress in expanding per capita manufacturing output was also made in Thailand and Malaysia. In Thailand, the 1960 level of per capita manufactures ($12.2) was well below the other non-stagnant Southeast Asian economies, but Thailand raised per capita manufactures by 123 per cent to $27.2 by 1968-70. Malaysia's per capita manufactures grew by 89 per cent during the 1960 decade, from $20.1 to $37.9. In the Philippines, where an import substitution strategy, biased against agriculture, had yielded rapid growth of manufacturing during the 1950s, progress during the 1960s was modest. Philippine per capita manufactures

Table 9

Manufacturing Value Added Per Capita[43]
(In U.S. Dollars of Current Purchasing Power)

Country	Manufacturing Value Added Per Capita 1960-62	1968-70	Decade Growth Rate (in percent)	Decade Real GDP Per Capita Growth Rate (in percent)
Burma	8.1	7.9[44]	- 2	1.0[44]
Indonesia	9.0	8.4	- 7	4.1
Malaysia, West	20.1	37.9	89	38.4
Philippines	25.5	32.9	29	23.1
Singapore	41.4	145.0	250	82.5
Thailand	12.2	27.2	123	62.9

[43]Value added in manufacturing: UN, Yearbook . . . (fn. 6).

Population: UN, Demographic Yearbook, (fn. 18).

Exchange Rates: IMF, International Financial Statistics, (fn. 13).

Real GDP Per Capita: See sources for Appendix A, Table A-2.

[44]1962-1970.

were raised by a mere 29 per cent over the decade, from $25.5 to $32.9. In the stagnant Southeast Asian economies, Burma's manufactures per capita fell by 2 per cent and Indonesia's by 7 per cent.

The final column in Table 9 shows the 1960 decade growth rate of real per capita GDP. It is apparent that there is a basic positive relationship between growth of manufactures per capita and growth of real GDP per capita. In the most rapidly growing dualistic economies (Thailand and Malaysia), growth of manufacturing substantially outpaced the growth of agriculture; while in the Philippines, which showed a more modest growth record, manufacturing grew slightly more rapidly than agriculture (see Table 8). These data do not undermine the validity of the strategy of balanced growth between agriculture and industry. Rather, they should be interpreted to demonstrate that where manufacturing is closely linked to agriculture, the growth of the manufacturing sector can induce relatively high rates of agricultural sector growth concomitant with manufacturing's expansion at even higher rates. It should be borne in mind, however, that the manufacturing sector's linkages with agriculture have remained predominantly in the export subsector.

IV. THE BROADER PERSPECTIVE

The transition from colonialism toward more modern, diversified growth systems was begun in Southeast Asian countries in the 1945-1960 period. After World War II, colonial-type restraints on national growth were gradually dissolved, but at varying rates, in Southeast Asian countries. Development planning for national, as distinct from colonial, objectives was introduced throughout Southeast Asia.

Between 1945 and 1960, significant differences in growth achievements appeared among Southeast Asian countries. Malaysia (then including Singapore), the Philippines, and Thailand had restored both export volume and per capita product to pre-World War II levels by 1950, and Malaysia and Thailand had recorded significant gains in both. During the 1950s, however, rapid growth and structural change occurred only in the Philippines, while Malaysia and Thailand showed little progress in remolding their inherited colonial economies or accelerating growth of exports and real output per capita.

Burma, Indonesia, and South Vietnam recovered slowly from the economic setbacks of World War II, and both export volume and, by 1960, per capita real product remained substantially below pre-war levels (Burma), or stagnated near the levels inherited from colonialism (Indonesia and South Vietnam). Genuine transition toward modern growth was stalled in these stagnant economies by political instability.

During the second decade after rehabilitation from World War II--the decade of the 1960s--new forces emerged to shape growth and development in Southeast Asia. Growing maturity of national governments led to more sophisticated and independent planning. Significant shifts occurred in development strategy, and greater haste in revamping the inherited colonial economies was evident. Singapore emerged on the scene in 1959 as an independent entity. After experimenting briefly with merger with Malaysia, Singapore went on to demonstrate a capacity for remarkable economic achievements as a city-state. In the mid-1960s, Indonesia gradually put its economic house in order for the first time in the postwar period and began to harness its resources for an assault on the problem of almost three decades of retrogression and stagnation. Burma, however, shifted increasingly toward a non-growth strategy, emphasizing withdrawal from world trade. Economic stagnation not only continued in Burma, but the beginnings toward transition growth during the 1950s were reversed.

Among the countries showing significantly positive per capita growth rates between 1960 and 1970, Singapore's performance clearly led the field, averaging increases of 6.2 per cent per year in per capita real product. Moreover, Singapore raised this growth rate from 2.5 per cent during the first half decade to 10.9 per cent in the second half. Thailand ranked second, raising per capita real product by 5 per cent per year, followed by Malaysia (3.3 per cent) and the Philippines (2.1 per cent). In Malaysia, performance in the second half decade lagged significantly behind performance in the first half decade, while the Philippines and Thailand performed somewhat better in the second half decade.

Viewed in the historical perspective of growth experience in contemporary advanced economies, the 1960s' record of the growing economies in Southeast Asia is quite remarkable. Simon Kuznets found that per capita real product growth rates in fourteen presently highly developed economies averaged from 10 to 30 per cent per decade, with 15 per cent per decade as a typically low limit.[45] Table 10 presents decade real per capita product and population growth rates for Southeast Asia. While stagnation is apparent for Burma, Indonesia and South Vietnam, the other countries performed well by historical standards of developed countries. The Philippines' performance on per capita real product over the 1960 decade

---

[45] Simon Kuznets, Modern Economic Growth: Rate, Structure and Spread (New Haven: Yale University Press, 1966), p. 67.

(23.1 per cent increase) was respectable in terms of Kuznets' long-run averages (10-30 per cent). The performance of Singapore (82.5 per cent increase) must be considered extraordinary in this historical perspective, while Thailand's progress (62.9 per cent increase) was also superior. Malaysia's decade rate of per capita real product growth (38.4 per cent increase) is also well above Kuznets' historical averages. These growth achievements are all the more remarkable in view of the rapid expansion of population during the 1960s. The rapid rates of population growth (shown in Table 10) greatly exceed those recorded during the transition to modern growth in advanced countries.[46] The accomplishments in the four growing economies (Malaysia, Philippines, Singapore, and Thailand) of overcoming high population growth rates and providing large increases in per capita real product suggest that a new growth era under transition from colonialism was launched during the 1960s.

The emergence of more rapid growth in Southeast Asia during the postwar transition than under colonialism is further confirmed by the longer time perspective shown in Table 11. The close relationship between Southeast Asia's indexes of per capita real product for 1937-1970, (shown in Column 1 and Asian LDC's Column 3) suggests that for pre-war and postwar growth comparisons we may use pre-war Asian performance as representative of Southeast Asia. Under this assumption, we find that the average annual growth rate of per capita real product for the pre-war period 1913-1937 was 1.3 per cent, while the Southeast Asian growth rate accelerated to 2.0 per cent in the 1950-1970 period (2.1 per cent for 1960-1970). Even during the heyday of colonialism, prior to 1929, the growth rate averaged only 1.5. This comparison should also be considered in terms of Indonesia's stagnation during the 1950-1970 period. Despite more than one half of Southeast Asia's weighted growth rate consisting of Indonesia's lagging performance (average annual growth rate of per capita real product = 1.0%), postwar progress in Southeast Asia substantially exceeded pre-war growth.

In the perspective of all non-Communist less-developed countries (Table 11, Column 2), Southeast Asia's transition growth performance (as well as non-Communist Asia as a whole) lagged behind the entire group. By 1970, Southeast Asia had raised per capita real product by 45 per cent above pre-war (1937), compared to a 72 per cent increase in all less-developed countries. Here, too, Indonesia's

---

[46] *Ibid.*, Chapter 2.

Table 10

1960 Decade Growth Rates: Per Capita Product In Constant Prices and Population[47] (In Percent)

Country	Per Capita Product	Population
Burma	1.0	23.1
Indonesia	4.1	29.3
Malaysia, West	38.4	34.4
Philippines	23.1	34.4
Singapore	82.5	28.0
Thailand	62.9	37.0
Vietnam, Republic	-4.0	26.8

[47] 10-year compound growth rates calculated from data in Appendix A, Table A-2. Republic of Vietnam data from UN, Yearbook . . . (fn. 6), various issues, adjusted.

Table 11

Indexes of Per Capita Real Product[48,49]
(1937 = 100)

Year	(1) Southeast Asia	(2) All LDC's[50]	(3) Asian LDC's[50]
1913	--	77	74
1929	--	93	94
1937	100	100	100
1950	97	107	97
1960	118	136	118
1970	145	172	146

[48] Southeast Asia (Column 1): See Table 3.

Other groupings (Columns 2 and 3): Derived from Bairoch, The Economic Development . . . (fn. 41), Chapter 10.

[49] All weighted by country population.

[50] Excludes Communist countries.

lagging performance accounts for Southeast Asia's inferior performance.

For the 1960 decade, when transition growth became firmly launched in Southeast Asia (excepting Burma and the Indochina countries), country comparisons with world groupings are possible for real product per capita and the major components of GDP. Table 12 presents growth rate estimates for GDP, GDP per capita, agricultural value added, industrial value added, and manufacturing value added--all in constant price (real) terms.

These comparative data highlight the exceptional performance of Singapore, Thailand, and Malaysia during the 1960s. Growth of GDP in these countries substantially exceeded averages shown for the entire world, developed market economies, and developing market economies. Despite high population growth rates in these Southeast Asian growth leaders, Singapore and Thailand out-performed all groupings on growth of per capita GDP while Malaysia's performance was exceeded only by developed market economies. The Philippines' performance on aggregate GDP was near the averages for all comparative groupings. Because of the Philippines' high population growth rate (3.0 per cent), however, per capita GDP growth was less than for any other grouping, developed or developing.

In agricultural growth, Malaysia, Thailand, and even the Philippines, showed substantially higher growth rates than any world grouping. In industrial and manufacturing growth, Singapore, Thailand, and Malaysia outperformed averages for all other groupings, while the Philippines' performance fell somewhat short of these groupings.

Performance in the stagnant Southeast Asian countries, Burma and Indonesia, fell substantially short of growth rate averages for the broader world groupings on all indicators--except for Burma's rate of agricultural growth, which slightly exceeded the averages of broader groupings.

Unweighted averages for Southeast Asian countries compare favorably with all larger groupings shown, and in the case of agriculture the average growth rate is substantially higher for Southeast Asia (4.1) than for the world (2.2), developed market economies (2.4), and developing market economies (2.7).

Weighted by country population, however, growth indicators for the Southeast Asia region as a whole lag behind those for other groups. This result is explained by the fact that 52 per cent of Southeast Asia's population in the countries shown was located in the stagnant economy of Indonesia.

Table 12

Average Annual Growth Rates, 1960-1970 GDP, GDP Per Capita, and Value Added in Agriculture, Industry, and Manufacturing (all in constant prices)

	GDP		Agri- culture	Industry	
	Total	Per Capita		Total[51]	Manu- facturing
World	5.6	3.5	2.2	6.7	NA
Market Economies	5.2	2.9	2.5	6.2	6.4
Developed Market Economies	5.2	4.0	2.4	6.0	6.3
Developing Market Economies	5.3	2.7	2.7	7.5	7.0
Southeast Asian Countries:					
Burma	2.3	0.1	2.8	3.0	3.3
Indonesia	3.0	0.4	2.1	4.3	3.3
Malaysia	6.3	3.3	6.0	7.8	10.2
Philippines	5.1	2.1	4.0	5.8	5.8
Singapore	9.8	6.2	--	14.0	14.5
Thailand	8.3	5.0	5.5	11.9	11.1
Southeast Asia, Averages:					
Unweighted	5.8	2.9	4.1	7.8	8.0
Weighted, by population	4.3	1.5	3.2	5.8	5.3

[51] Industry as defined in footnote 29, Table 7.

Postscript on Indonesia's Recent Growth

We have seen that despite the evidence substantiating a new stage of transition growth in Southeast Asia, the area's comparative performance from 1937-1970 was severely hampered by relative stagnation in the most populous country, Indonesia.

Indonesia is Southeast Asia's largest country, and her population of over 130 million represents approximately one half of the region's total population. The combination of the large, potentially productive labor force and Indonesia's diversified natural resource base present the possibility of Indonesia's becoming Southeast Asia's dominant economy.

During the first two decades of independence (1949-1970), however, the Indonesian economy showed little progress. Per capita product in 1970 remained near the level achieved under colonialism in the late 1930s. The output and employment structure of the domestic economy remained essentially stagnant, and the manufacturing sector (both as a share of total product and in per capita output) remained among the smallest in Southeast Asia. Indonesia began the transition with serious handicaps, compared to the Southeast Asian countries where transition experience has been more successful. Colonialism left a large and backward agricultural sector where population pressure on land was much more severe than elsewhere in Southeast Asia. The export enclave (including both export production and related activities) was a smaller component of total output and more isolated from the economic activity of the bulk of the indigenous population in traditional agriculture. The sharp dualism fostered by Dutch colonialism was also reflected in the government bureaucracy. Dutch control extended far down the civil service ladder, and opportunities for training and experience in government were meager.

While indigenous entrepreneurial capacity to maintain the crucial growth functions in the inherited enclave sector of the economy was lacking, Indonesia's initial transition strategy (1950-1964) called for an aggressive program of import substitution. Originally designed to stimulate industrial investment by private entrepreneurs through lenient provision of public credit and foreign exchange allocations, the program shifted toward public control in the industrial sector during the 1950s. Lacking entrepreneurship for import substitution growth through either policy, the strain of this unrealistic strategy eventually caused excessively high rates of inflation and falling levels of output throughout the economy.

Retrogression continued from the late 1950s until the new political regime came to power in 1965.

The post-1965 government adopted growth objectives more appropriate to Indonesia's acute shortage of indigenous entrepreneurship. Initial emphasis centered upon restoration of relative economic stability, fuller utilization of existing productive capacity throughout the economy, and recovery of primary product exports. A realistic strategy for transition growth was adopted near the end of the period under review. The present strategy focuses upon promoting export growth through development of Indonesia's natural resources by reliance upon foreign investment, introducing modern inputs into the backward traditional agricultural sector, and expanding the economy's social overhead capital to accommodate growth in all of the economy's key sectors. While this composite strategy has positive effects on increasing Indonesia's entrepreneurial capacity, more direct and vigorous policies to encourage entrepreneurial development remain a chief requisite for more successful transition growth in Indonesia.

During the first half of the 1970 decade (1970-75), the Indonesian economy has reversed the stagnation trend apparent from 1949 to 1965. The reorientation of growth strategy after 1965 provided preconditions for this turnabout. Even before the dramatic improvement in Indonesia's terms of trade associated with the petroleum price boom,[52] growth in domestic sectors showed a sharp acceleration. Aggregate real product grew at an average annual rate of 7.5 per cent from 1970 to 1973, by 11.7 per cent in 1973 and 7.5 per cent in 1974. As a result, per capita real product rose by 29 per cent between 1970 and 1974 (at an annual average rate of 5.3 per cent). This growth performance in the 1970s was second only to Singapore in Southeast Asia.

In view of the difficulties in launching transition growth in Indonesia between independence (1949) and 1970, the danger of Indonesia reverting to her earlier stagnation trend must be recognized. If the new growth momentum can be maintained, however, Southeast Asia's prospects for becoming a major center of economic power will be greatly enhanced. Indonesia is a giant in population,

---

[52] Increased world prices for petroleum exports have had a dramatic effect on Indonesia's export earnings. Crude petroleum export prices rose by 58 per cent in 1972, by 36 per cent in 1973 and by 207 per cent in 1974. From 1971 to 1974, Indonesia's export earnings rose from U.S. $1.2 billion to U.S. $7.5 billion, with petroleum exports rising from 46 per cent to 72 per cent of the total. (Data from IMF, <u>International Financial Statistics</u>, (fn. 13).)

ranking fifth in the world. If this massive potential labor force can be equipped with modern capital goods and technology, Indonesia may outpace Japan in Asia's economic leadership within the next several decades. Indonesia's wealth of natural resources, particularly minerals and petroleum, suggest that the possibility of modernization on the large scale required to push Indonesia to economic leadership in Asia may indeed be feasible from the resource viewpoint. If this is to occur, however, revolutionary improvements in human resource development and entrepreneurship are essential.

REGIONAL COOPERATION IN SOUTHEAST ASIA: IMPLICATIONS FOR WORLD LEADERSHIP

Amado A. Castro

A few years ago at a gathering similar to this, I noted that Southeast Asia's share in world trade had declined in the postwar period compared to pre-World War II and that Southeast Asia had declined in relative economic importance. It was a statement of fact, but the paper ended with a hope and indeed an expectation that the trend would be reversed and that sub-regional economic cooperation would assist in reversing the trend. Since 1972, when my paper was written, the political and economic situation in Southeast Asia has changed in ways that may bring about a fulfillment of my hopes and predictions, even though at this point those sanguine prospects are still a long way from fruition.

In 1938 the eleven countries of Southeast Asia accounted for 3.7 per cent of world exports and in 1948 for 4.5 per cent; then slowly this share declined to 2.1 per cent in 1971. But before going further, it may be useful to note where things have not changed. Economic growth, though held down by the recession in the advanced countries, has continued, at a rate (3.1 per cent for per capita GDP) generally higher than in the other underdeveloped regions of Africa and Latin America, and with world economic recovery there is every expectation that economic growth will rise to even higher levels than before the recession.

In many important ways conditions in Southeast Asia have changed for the better. First of all, there is the military situation. Perhaps the most important change is the end of the Indochina conflicts. This has reduced the number of Southeast Asian countries from eleven to ten as Vietnam has been united *de facto* and is soon to be united by law. Peace in Indochina should enable the victorious governments of Vietnam, Cambodia, and Laos to rehabilitate their economies and develop them. The withdrawal of American forces from Thailand has meant the end of one particular expansionary force in that country, and at the same time an increase in political and military insecurity and instability. But if I may be allowed to make a guess or perhaps express a hope, it would seem that Thailand has enough resilience as a nation to cope with such problems. In another part of Southeast Asia, the Philippines, the Muslim secessionist movement is more or less contained, especially as support for the insurgents coming through Sabah seems to have been curtailed or cut off, although the rebellion is not completely settled. The decline (though not eradication) of armed conflict in Southeast Asia should mean that more resources and energies can now be turned to political development and economic growth.

As has been mentioned, the forces for economic growth present before the world recession of 1974-75 should re-emerge with recovery. Furthermore it is fair to say that improvements in organization and management of economic resources have been proceeding continuously in many of the nations of Southeast Asia, especially the ASEAN members--Indonesia, Malaysia, the Philippines, Singapore, and Thailand. Manpower training and education, a crucial area in which Southeast Asia countries are generally ahead of most LDC's, have been expanding and deepening. While population growth remains high, it has slowed down somewhat--dramatically in Singapore, perceptibly in the Philippines.

On the whole, prospects for the economic future of Southeast Asia appear to be favorable; the conspicuous exceptions seem to be Burma and Cambodia. However for purposes of assessing the future economic influence of Southeast Asia, it may be appropriate to narrow somewhat the field of view of this paper. Burma may be excluded from consideration as it continues its self-imposed policy of withdrawal from world affairs. As for Indochina, the countries of Vietnam, Cambodia, and Laos may likewise be left out as they are engrossed in nation-building with an inward focus, albeit apparently along different paths.

Such considerations leave the five members of ASEAN--the Association of Southeast Asian Nations--as the only outward-looking Southeast Asian countries which will have some influence on the rest of the world. This is not to imply that what happens in Burma or what the Indochinese nations do will not be meaningful to the rest of the world, only that such events will have less direct significance than will the actions of a group of nations that have a policy of behaving in a world context. This is certainly true in regard to economic affairs but might be less so in political matters.

ASEAN Economic Cooperation

The five member nations of ASEAN--Indonesia, Malaysia, the Philippines, Singapore, Thailand--hold a population of 227 million (1972); this is a population larger than that of the United States. Indonesia, the largest at 130 million, is the fifth most populous nation in the world, and the Philippines and Thailand are fifteenth and sixteenth respectively with 42 and 41 million. Yet this five-nation grouping only produced total GNP of $27.4 billion in 1969, which compared with $29.2 billion for Norway and Sweden and Australia-New Zealand, $39.5 billion for India, $37.5 billion for Belgium and the Netherlands, $50 billion for Canada, $44.9 billion for all Africa and $102.6 billion for Latin America and the Carribbean. Two of the ASEAN members (Malaysia and Thailand) are located on the mainland of Asia, while the other three (Indonesia, the Philippines, and Singapore) are island nations detached from the mainland, though Singapore is somewhat less so.

Perhaps some idea of the relative diversity of the grouping is given by contrasting the two largest nations--Indonesia and the Philippines and also the smallest, Singapore. Indonesia and the Philippines together account for 75 per cent of the population of ASEAN and have the largest GNP. Despite the fact that Indonesia has over three times the population of the Philippines, the difference in GDP between the two is small, only $1.6 billion (Indonesia--US$15.9 billion in 1974, Philippines--US$14.3 billion). Value added in manufacturing in the Philippines is actually higher--$3.1 billion as against $1.6 billion for Indonesia. Since 1972 Indonesia has had four more years of competent management of her economy, and economic growth rates, currently the highest in Southeast Asia after Singapore, show this. As for the Philippines, almost four years of constitutional authoritarianism in government have meant visible progress in reform and improvement of the governmental machinery, building up of infrastructure, agricultural advance including land reform, regional development, attraction of foreign capital, and many other aspects of economic and political, not to mention cultural, life. The recent discovery of oil which seems to be in commercial quantities should ease balance of payment pressures besides opening up a needed energy resource. Singapore, the smallest economy, covers 225 square miles of area with a population of 2.2 million and GNP of $3.3 billion, but it has the highest per capita GNP of $1,490 and the largest per capita value added in manufacturing. The other two ASEAN nations, Thailand and Malaysia, are somewhere between the other three in terms of industrial development.

Despite such diversity, as well as the low level of intra-regional trade up to this time, there are advantages foreseen from economic cooperation. In 1970-72 a United Nations team, at the request of the ASEAN, made a study of ASEAN economic cooperation, turning in its report in mid-1972. In that report a number of benefits from economic cooperation were cited. The chief of these was enlargement of the market and the economies of scale and possibilities of specialization arising from this. The report showed the savings in capital requirements as well as costs of production possible if manufacturing faculties were constructed for the whole grouping rather than for even the largest of the national markets.

Besides the economic gains from economies of scale, one more might be mentioned, a political-economic reason for cooperation which I have often cited. It might be termed a defense and self-preservation argument: if the ASEAN nations do not unite, they will be subject to pressures and perhaps domination, both political and economic, from the big powers in this world: the United States, Russia, China, India, Japan. Even a scheme such as the neutralization of ASEAN, which some proponents feel could be one way to avoid big power domination, cannot be achieved unless the ASEAN nations, individually and collectively, are strong; weakness is only an invitation to attempts at dominance. And then there is a new factor that has arisen with the unification of Vietnam: whether or not it is deliberately fomented, there will inevitably be competition, open or disguised, political, military, and/or economic, between this potentially powerful but socialist-oriented nation and the more private enterprise-oriented and open economies of its neighbors.

It is therefore heartening that at the recent Bali summit of the heads of the five ASEAN members last February, some consensus seems to have been reached that the time has come to promote more active regional economic cooperation. This is a promising change of direction in the relations between the members as it would seem that economic cooperation is easier to achieve and can lead to more concrete results than political and cultural cooperation. Such at any rate seems to be the guiding principle and experience in the European Economic Community: that economic cooperation is the more promising and productive prelude to eventual political union. Nevertheless there are many difficulties and unresolved questions in ASEAN economic cooperation.

The principal forms of ASEAN economic cooperation proposed by the United Nations team in 1972 were trade liberalization, complementation arrangements, and package deals. Other forms mentioned were monetary and clearing arrangements, methods of financing development, and insurance; also research services, cooperation in ancillary services such as shipping and tourism, and coordination of national economic plans.

The first three proposals were clearly the more important and potentially most far-reaching. Trade liberalization was to take the form principally of tariff preferences for each others' goods on a selective basis. Complementation arrangements meant that the member countries were to choose industries, with different countries setting up facilities to produce different components of the product, and then exchanging these components freely among each other. Using automobiles as an example, one country would be the site for a stamping plant, another for a foundry for engine blocks, a third for a transmission factory, a fourth for interior trim, and the fifth for rear axles and differentials. The parts would be shipped to each country where the complete automobile would be assembled.

As for the third proposal, package deals, the ASEAN study group examined a number of industrial products--looked over the national markets and the combined regional one, computed the capital and unit costs of setting up plants to produce these products in each country and then for the region as a whole. Now the ingenious part of the "package deal" proposal was the provision that the five ASEAN members would agree to choose, say, five products, assign one to each of the member countries, possibly jointly finance and own them, and then extend reciprocal trade privileges on these products. As one would expect, there were substantial capital and operating economies from setting up single plants to serve the entire region. The products included nitrogenous fertilizer, phosphate fertilizer, carbon black, soda ash, caprolactam, newsprint, sheet glass, small internal combustion engines, electrical compressors, typewriters, and others. The proposals were not necessarily grounded on government participation or ownership but in fact private enterprise participation was welcomed.

The progress along the three proposed lines of cooperation since the ASEAN Study mission turned in its report has been spotty. In the first place for some reason the ASEAN Study Group Report was regarded as confidential; only a few copies were printed. Instead of being disseminated widely as one would expect so as to build up support, the report was limited in circulation. Yet the United Nations headquarters itself published the report as its *Journal of Development Planning*, No. 7 (1974), thus presumably removing any confidentiality to the report.

In 1974, at meetings in Manila, representatives of the five ASEAN members met and seemed to have made some forward movement when they agreed to examine possible trade liberalization in perhaps 100 food products. There were also meetings of officials at which the Philippine Progressive Car Manufacturing Program (PCMP) was examined as a possible model for complementation in automobile manufacturing. Possibilities of complementation in other products, such as in refrigerators and air conditioners, were looked into.

In the private sector, meetings of ASEAN national Chambers of Commerce propagated the idea of cooperation among private businessmen. For example, it was reported that sheet glass producers in the Philippines and Thailand agreed not to duplicate production facilities but to specialize in particular types of sheet glass and exchange them. Government officials were said to be receptive to specialization such as this and were prepared to support it with tariff liberalization and similar measures.

Undoubtedly, the biggest recent impetus for ASEAN cooperation has been the summit meeting of the heads of State of the five ASEAN nations in Bali on February 23-24. The results of the preparatory meetings for the summit had seemed discouraging with regard to ASEAN economic cooperation. Singapore and the Philippines proposed across the board tariff reductions among the ASEAN members of, say, 10 or 20 per cent. Indonesia objected, causing a bombshell and discouragement; it argued that being less developed industrially than the other nations, any precipitate tariff preferences would prevent her own industries from developing and would propagate her relative underdevelopment. The argument is perfectly understandable and one can sympathize with it. Not being privy to the considerations behind the Singapore and Philippines proposal, one can only make surmises about why the proposal was advanced in the form it was; perhaps it was intended as a grand gesture to demonstrate vividly the determination of the ASEAN nations to move trade cooperation forward. Yet it would seem that some economists failed to appreciate the natural reaction of Indonesia or any other ASEAN nation that for some reason perceived itself as lagging behind the others. After all the ASEAN study group anticipated the objection and carefully made clear that what it proposed in trade liberalization was <u>selective</u> measures, not across the board tariff cuts. News reports have indicated that Indonesia feared Singapore as the advanced industrial nation, but this fear is misplaced: Singapore is too small in population and its potentials as an industrial center are limited by this fact. I suspect that the Indonesians were more apprehensive, and with reason, about the Philippine manufacturing sector which is the largest and most advanced on a wide front within ASEAN.

Whatever may be the progress with regard to trade liberalization, whether selective or across the board, at this time the most immediately promising avenue of ASEAN economic cooperation after the Bali summit seems to be, paradoxically, package deals. This is paradoxical because it appeared to be the most difficult to achieve of the three, requiring the most preparation, bargaining, and minute discussion of details. Yet in fact it seems to have been the easiest for the five ASEAN leaders to understand, appreciate, and agree upon in principle. And so meetings have been held since the Bali summit to hammer down details of the package deals, apparently to locate an ASEAN area fertilizer plant in Indonesia, a phosphate fertilizer plant in the Philippines, a diesel engine manufacturing facility in Singapore, and so on.

The Bali summit, in terms of specifics spelled out in a communique, may not have accomplished any immediately dramatic steps forward, but it seems that a consensus was reached by the five leaders about a number of points; and in Asian terms, this means a lot. And so there may now be real determination to get ASEAN economic cooperation going in earnest.

Unresolved Issues

However, there are still a number of issues regarding the schemes of cooperation which do not seem to be clear as yet and which will have to be tackled or defined in detail in meetings of the economics ministers of the member nations.

To begin with, while the package deals will probably go forward now, what about the two other forms of cooperation, namely, trade liberalization and complementation? Trade liberalization on the basis of an across the board tariff reduction seems to have been scuttled by an Indonesian veto. But it bears repeating that the ASEAN Study Group set up by the United Nations had recommended a product-by-product approach. This is sensible as well as feasible: there are a number of industrial products which are turned out in each or in most of the ASEAN countries and where competence has been achieved: rubber tires, sanitary wares, refrigerators, sheet glass, and others. For example in tires, perhaps the Philippines could specialize in producing 15-inch tires which go into Volkswagen Beetles, as there is a large demand for these in the Philippines, while another country could specialize in 14-inch tires which go on Renaults and Mercedes-Benzes of which there are not many in the Philippines. Then these tires could be exchanged freely between the two countries. Or again, the sheet glass producers of the Philippines and Thailand have indicated how they could each specialize. It should also be remembered that two years ago, technical committee meetings led to agreement to examine possible trade liberalization in approximately 100 categories of food.

Complementation is another promising method of cooperation, but the difficulties may be illustrated with regard to automobile manufacturing. The automobile example is at once dramatic as it is a highly visible form of manufacturing activity to which many countries aspire, but at the same time it is not quite a typical area of complementation as it is a somewhat more complicated case than, say, refrigerators or air conditioners. Be that as it may, complementation in automotive manufacturing may deserve examination. An appropriate starting point for discussion may be the Philippine Progressive Car Manufacturing Program (PCMP). Under this plan, only five firms have been allowed to assemble and market automobiles in the Philippines; the limit was imposed because of the small size of the domestic market. There is a requirement for increasing use of locally-made components in the automobiles, up to 50 per cent; however, exports of locally-produced components count towards the local content requirement. Every year the market performance of the participants in the program is reviewed and their foreign exchange allocations are adjusted. One of the criteria in the choice of the participants in the program was the possibility of coordinating their local manufacturing with a regional complementation scheme. The Philippine PCMP therefore offers a basis for ASEAN complementation in automotive manufacturing. Already the PCMP has inspired a plan by an independent American component manufacturer to produce automotive differentials and rear axles using parts turned out in three plants located in the Philippines, Malaysia, and Thailand. One advantage worth pointing out with regard to ASEAN complementation in car manufacture is that given the technical skills required as well as the large scales of production which call for large capital investments, foreign investors from outside the region will have to be involved.

But there are difficulties in getting complementation in car manufacturing going. What is perhaps the biggest obstacle can be shown by reference to the Philippine program. Before the Philippine PCMP was put into effect, much opposition from consumers desiring a wider choice of products and the vested interests of the car manufacturers then on the market had to be overcome. Would the other ASEAN countries besides the Philippines be disposed to accept the narrowing of consumer choice and the resolute discipline and economic controls which the Philippines has imposed on its car manufacturers and car buyers? It is a valid question whether the publics and the decision makers in the other ASEAN countries would consider the sacrifices worthwhile and acceptable.

It is sobering to note however that whether or not ASEAN will act to promote regional car complementation, it is in fact happening already--but on a north-south basis, not on an ASEAN foundation. For example, it seems that Ford Motor Company has formulated plans to set up different manufacturing facilities in Korea, Taiwan, the Philippines, and Australia--engines are already being produced in Taiwan and body stampings in the Philippines.

It may well be that the ASEAN countries will not make the decisions or take the steps to promote automotive complementation in the ASEAN region, but on the other hand, who can rule out the possibility that the decision makers might agree on such a step at some future summit meeting? Perhaps too, even though car complementation would be a highly visible example of ASEAN economic cooperation, complementation might be more feasible in a smaller, less prominent industry such as air conditioners or refrigerators.

The last unresolved issue that might be mentioned here is the attitude towards and the role of foreign, that is, non-ASEAN investors. All the ASEAN member nations are now, vocally and in fact, openly receptive to foreign investors. But there will have to be discussion of and agreement on a number of questions with regard to foreign investors, with the end in view of framing a reasonably consistent and substantially uniform policy for ASEAN. Among these questions are uniform investment incentives among all the ASEAN countries so as to avoid needless competition; identification by each country and for the region as a whole of the areas in which foreign participation will be allowed; a definition or delineation of the roles of the public sector and private enterprises; the extent of local as against foreign contribution, and so on.

Implications of ASEAN Economic Cooperation

By now it is generally accepted within the region that ASEAN cooperation is desirable, nay, even necessary and it is heartening for an economist that the economic and business aspects of cooperation are being pushed to the forefront instead of being neglected. It is finally realized that economic cooperation can lead to concrete and significant benefits more quickly and easily than political, cultural, and other forms of cooperation. The economic benefits of regional cooperation and a wider market, as pointed out in the textbooks and confirmed from experience in other parts of the world, can also be expected in ASEAN. The self-defense aspect--that united the ASEAN countries stand whereas divided they fall--is appreciated.

But what would the new thrust of ASEAN economic cooperation mean for the rest of the world? First, there are features of the projected cooperation that are of interest. The ASEAN members have demonstrated not only determination but also realism--recognition that some countries among them have special economic problems, that some lag behind others in stage of development--and a willingness to accommodate to these differences while still moving towards cooperation. New methods of economic cooperation are being tried or considered--specifically, package deals and complementation, and the experience with these in ASEAN might be instructive for other on-going or proposed regional blocs. It should be reassuring to many that the ASEAN countries favor private enterprise in their economic orientation; they look to private enterprise to carry the main thrust of the business cooperation in the region, with the governments setting the stage and supporting the private business efforts, though also carrying out industrial ventures when necessary or appropriate. And the ASEAN nations are not hostile to foreign (i.e., non-regional) investors; indeed the governments welcome foreigners as partners in and contributors to development.

The biggest anticipated effect of ASEAN cooperation would be to strengthen not only the individual countries but also the region as a whole. The rest of the world has an interest in a strong Southeast Asia. Japan has a particular stake in a stable ASEAN. Southeast Asia is her biggest market, absorbing 25 per cent of Japan's exports in 1971 and a source of many of her raw materials--accounting for 16 per cent of Japan's imports in 1971. Through the Straits of Malacca pass 90 per cent of Japan's oil imports and large volumes of her exports and other imports, especially to Europe. The United States is farther away, but nonetheless ASEAN is important; again as a market and a source of raw materials. Historically the United States has run balance of trade deficits with Southeast Asia. It is also as a region which is sympathetic in ideology to American ideals and goals. As for Australia, her re-orientation towards Asia rather than Europe is inevitable, and Southeast Asia is the part of Asia that is closest to her. All of Australia's trade with the other advanced economies of Japan and Europe must pass through ASEAN territory.

Above all, there is the significance and contribution to the world that can be made by the ASEAN grouping of 230 million people--a population larger than the United States' and approaching the USSR's, and comparable to Africa's or Latin America's. In general these five nations, which have been growing faster than Africa and Latin America, are already at an intermediate level of economic development. They are clearly potential achievers and will reach a stage of advanced economic development sooner than many other less developed countries. It should be in the interest of the rest of the world, especially the advanced nations of the first world, to actively support ASEAN economic cooperation and development.

COMMENTS AND CONCLUSIONS ON THE ECONOMIC PAPERS

Lawrence D. Stifel

The authors of the three papers presented at this panel, Professors Golay, Castro, and Paauw, are distinguished senior economists, whose professional careers have been devoted in various ways to understanding and strengthening the economies of Southeast Asia. Space is not available here to describe their individual contributions, which have included pioneering research and writing over a period of about two decades on the economic development of the region, training of American and Asian graduate students on the economy of the region, development of the leading graduate educational programs in the United States and Southeast Asia for teaching and research on Southeast Asia, and direct participation as advisors and in other capacities with economic development agencies in the region. All three have a special professional interest in the Philippines. During his tenure as Dean of the School of Economics, University of the Philippines, Dr. Castro built the institution into a strong regional economics center which continues to attract graduate students from all over the region and whose staff and graduates are actively involved in improving economic policy and performance in the region. The two Americans, Drs. Golay and Paauw, have served as visiting professors at the School of Economics and have written about the Philippine economy. At the same time, all three have a long-standing record of professional concern and involvement with other countries of the region and the region as a whole that uniquely qualifies them to address the question posed in the title of this panel.

The analysis and conclusions in the three papers are sound and reasonable as one would expect from these three scholars. But while each paper is relevant to an understanding of the economic future of Southeast Asia, because of the nature of the assigned topics, each standing alone is incomplete. The objectives of the following comments, therefore, will be to identify the most critical variables and attempt to focus them in an integrated way on the question of whether Southeast Asia is an emerging center of economic influence.

According to Professor Golay, the countries of Southeast Asia are small powers and their potential to aggregate power through economic cooperation and integration is limited by the similarity of their economic structures. In the static sense, the region's lack of economic significance is incontrovertible. This is evident in the selected statistics presented in Table 1. With something over 300 million people, Southeast Asia has roughly 8 per cent of the world's population. The gross regional product, in contrast, is probably no more than 1 per cent of the gross world product. This implies that the countries of the region are very poor indeed. The judgment, however, is one applicable to the entire Third World. It underscores the poverty of the developing countries without illuminating which countries or regions have the economic potential and political determination to achieve an adequate level and quality of economic growth.

Cutting across the region's extraordinary cultural and political diversity is the economic legacy produced by each country's common experience with Western colonialism. In spite of the similarities in their economic underpinnings described by Golay, the countries in the region have evolved into two political-economic blocs, the market economies of ASEAN and the communist states of Indochina, with Burma as a stagnant backwater seeking its own independent destiny. The primary focus of the second and third papers is the ASEAN group, perhaps because we know more about these countries or because they are considered to have the greater potential as "an emerging center of economic influence."

Golay's rather pessimistic assessment of the region's power has sufficient realism to serve as a useful antidote to the naive belief that the wealth of the tropics can be easily unlocked if the right keys are identified. He does not draw the reasonable conclusion that recognition of these facts of life is the first stage for realistic economic planning. Miracle seeds or discoveries of oil may provide temporary relief, but they cannot substitute for a sustained national commitment to the difficult task of transforming poor and traditional societies.

Golay's analysis properly identifies the population problem, particularly in relation to the frontier of land suitable for cultivation. The growth of food production in much of the region has been accomplished by an expansion of area with relatively unchanged technology, except for the areas planted with the high yielding grain varieties. Southeast Asia is primarily agrarian, with a majority of the population in the rural areas, but agriculture generally receives a small proportion of the investment resources and support from the central government. Productivity in this traditional sector is lagging behind that in the service and industrial sectors.

Professor Paauw's paper shows that agricultural production, weighted by population (ASEAN plus Burma), grew during the last decade at 3.2 per cent. By historical standards this is a commendable achievement--a rate of growth about double that

Table 1

Selected Statistics on Southeast Asia

	1974 Population (millions)[1]	1972 Gross Domestic Product (billions)[3]
ASEAN COUNTRIES		
Thailand	41.0	$ 7.7
Philippines	41.5	8.6
Indonesia	127.6	11.0
Singapore	2.2	2.9
Malaysia	11.6	4.0
Total ASEAN	223.9	34.2
Burma	30.3	2.0
INDOCHINA		
Cambodia	7.9	0.9[2]
Laos	3.3	0.2[2]
North Vietnam	23.2	3.5
South Vietnam	18.3[2]	2.6
Total Indochina	52.7	7.2
TOTAL SOUTHEAST ASIA	306.9	43.4
COMPARATIVE STATISTICS		
Japan	109.7	$ 375
Developed non-Communist Countries		$2,920
Less Developed non-Communist Countries		469
Communist Countries		1,070
WORLD TOTAL	3,890	$4,460

[1] United Nations, Department of Economic and Social Affairs, Statistical Office, Statistical Yearbook, 1975 (New York: United Nations, 1976), pp. 70-1.

[2] For the year 1970.

[3] With the exception of North Vietnam, statistics on Southeast Asia are from the U.N., Statistical Yearbook, 1975, (fn. 1), p. 702. GDP for North Vietnam is crudely estimated by multiplying the population times $150. Other GDP data are from U.S. Central Intelligence Agency, Handbook of Economic Statistics, 1975 (Washington, D.C.: Government Printing Office, 1975), p. 29.

of the United States since the Civil War. By the urgent standards of the region's growing population it is inadequate. Paauw provides evidence that per capita physical production, measured in calories per farm worker, has fallen in Indonesia and the Philippines since 1950, in spite of the "green revolution." Moreover, these farm workers have to support even more nonagricultural workers now than before. Only in Thailand has the per capita production increased, presumably because of the surplus land available there. According to United Nations estimates, in 1971 the high yielding varieties of rice accounted for 50 per cent of planted area in the Philippines, 25 per cent in West Malaysia, and 11 per cent in Indonesia.[4] There were off-setting factors which dragged total yields down in spite of the impact of the high yielding varieties. Moreover there is evidence that the annual rate of increased production is declining as the most favorable areas for planting the new seeds are exploited. The next stages of growth in agriculture would seem to require substantially larger investments in rural infrastructure, especially irrigation and roads, as well as improved systems for the provision of inputs and distribution of production. In the Asian Development Bank's study, Southeast Asian Economy in the 1970s, Hla Myint stated that the "green revolution" could be the central force in the region's economic development.[5] The use of the new varieties will more resemble a minor coup than a revolution unless the countries of the region place higher priority on the agricultural sector to institutionalize agricultural modernization.

Projections of the region's population over the next quarter century suggest the staggering demands to be placed on the regional economy--a doubling of population under the most optimistic assumptions. Increased agricultural productivity is necessary to provide a reprieve from these demands until effective programs to reduce population growth can be implemented. There is encouraging evidence that birth rates are starting to decline now in some ASEAN countries, thus creating hope that the region may be able to escape the Malthusian specter in the long run.

Paauw's assessment of ASEAN's economic growth in the 1960s is more favorable and his view of the future more optimistic than would appear warranted by Golay's paper. Paauw's conclusions have special interest because they differ sharply from his

---

[4]United Nations, Economic and Social Commission for Asia and the Pacific, Economic and Social Survey of Asia and the Pacific 1974 (Bangkok: United Nations Publication, 1975), p. 76.

[5]Asian Development Bank, Southeast Asia's Economy in the 1970s (London: Longman, 1971), pp. 5-17.

important earlier study, "Economic Progress in Southeast Asia," published in 1963.[6] A portion of the final paragraph of that article can usefully be reproduced here because it had significant influence upon intellectual thought at that time and can illuminate changes that have occurred over the last decade:

> One can hardly view with equanimity the rising rate of population growth in both growing and stagnant economies. Confronted with this drag on raising per capita real income, no Southeast Asian country has succeeded in raising the rate of growth of aggregate real product over the course of the postwar period. On the contrary it appears that there has been a perceptible retardation of growth rates in all Southeast Asian countries, and where new growth has occurred it appears that incremental capital-output ratios have risen sharply. In short, there has been a tendency for the slow-growth economies to grow less rapidly--both in terms of aggregate and per capita product. As the task of rehabilitation has been completed in some countries or prolonged in others, the growth momentum originally provided from output gains in the sectors most responsive to mere restoration of political and social stability has petered out. The mushrooming of economic plans throughout the area and the conscious application of public policy to promote growth have failed to reverse the trend toward a narrowing gap between growth of output and growth of population. The question should at least be raised as to whether these economies may not be tending to revert toward the underdeveloped state where the equilibrium growth rate is zero after experiencing a period of growth induced by favorable external stimuli during the immediate postwar period.

What factors explain the difference in Paauw's conclusions in 1963 and 1976? One can reject the hypothesis that the change is a statistical illusion. Although Paauw's analysis is based primarily on the aggregate statistical data, there is probably no economist more familiar with the conceptual and empirical inadequacies of the economic data in the ASEAN region--nor more sensitive to the limitation in their use. The validity of these conclusions is further strengthened by Paauw's firsthand experience in the ASEAN countries over a period of several decades.

Paauw's first article, quoted above, was based largely on the experience of the 1950s, the first decade after rehabilitation from the damage of World War II. Significant growth and structural change had occurred only in the Philippines by that time. Paauw's optimism in the present paper is based upon the strong economic record in the 1960s of Singapore, Thailand, Malaysia, and--after 1965--of Indonesia. During the second decade after the wartime rehabilitation, there was evidence that

---

[6] Douglas S. Paauw, "Economic Progress in Southeast Asia," Journal of Asian Studies, 23 (November 1963), p. 90.

all the ASEAN countries were in a process of transition from colonial-type economies. Paauw's revised judgment is formed on the basis of developments during a relatively brief period of time. Before considering whether those favorable trends are likely to continue in the future--whether Southeast Asia is an emerging center of economic influence--several observations on the paper seem warranted:

1. Paauw's framework of analysis skillfully orders diverse and enormous quantities of raw data. However, it may suggest greater explanatory and predictive power than is warranted. The positive correlation, for example, between economic variables such as exports and growth does not prove causality. There may be other, more complex and hidden factors affecting growth. The analysis does not explain why exports grew in the 1960s nor, of course, how to promote them in the future.

2. The concept that countries deliberately adopt particular national growth strategies may not be completely realistic. National policies in Southeast Asia are seldom so rational or coherent. Building roads in Northeastern Thailand for security purposes, for example, opened up new farmland, thus indirectly promoting the diversification of agricultural exports. Ex post facto, this has been characterized as an export promotion strategy. This observation is not meant to deny the value of attempting to identify or implement national economic strategies that will improve the coherence of economic decision-making.

3. Rapid economic growth rates are a necessary but not a sufficient condition of improved social welfare. Neither Paauw nor the other writers consider how the benefits of economic growth have been distributed among different social classes. Although the panel was not asked directly to address the issue of social justice, it is relevant because the legitimacy of the economic system depends upon some minimum level of public support. There is growing criticism in the ASEAN countries that the poor and powerless are not sharing in the type of growth that these free-market economies are producing.

There is little objective evidence that economic growth has worsened the overall distribution of income in any ASEAN country. Rising income has clearly not reduced the income gap between the urban centers and the countryside, but there are signs of improvement in most rural areas. The rise in life expectancy is the most significant index of increased welfare. More conspicuous signs in many villages are consumer goods such as corrugated steel roofing, transistor radios, and bicycles that were not available a decade or so ago. Equal distribution of growth, of course, increases the absolute size of the gap between the rich and the poor, and this permits a style of life in the capitals that appears inequitable in such poor countries. Moreover, the large profits arising out of the private enterprise system and the corruption made possible by the expansion of government expenditures have contributed to conspicuous extravagances that generate resentment and alienation. This is not to deny that poverty is real and oppressive for the poorest classes, the unemployed in the cities, and the underemployed in the villages. These groups, however, pose less of a political risk than the students and others in the middle who develop a sense of relative deprivation arising out of the growth process.

Paauw's objective is to deepen understanding of the postwar economic development of the ASEAN group of nations. He neither prescribes nor predicts the future. The statistical analysis essentially ends at 1970 and there is no attempt to assess the impact of the three shocks to the international economy that occurred about 1973--the food crisis, the energy crisis, and the worldwide inflation. In the aggregate data, Indonesia, the fifth largest nation in the world, dominates the ASEAN performance. Paauw suggests that success in the 1970s and 1980s will depend upon whether Indonesia can sustain its post-1965 growth rate in spite of these economic shocks, and whether the manufacturing sector in all countries can transmit the growth impetus to traditional agriculture, thus overcoming the historic dualism in their economic structures.

Professor Castro is optimistic about the economic prospects of the region and the ability of the ASEAN countries to strengthen their economies through regional cooperation. He notes that the ASEAN summit meeting held February 1976 in Bali may represent a critical transition point in shifting from a first stage of ASEAN development lasting nine years, in which the emphasis has been primarily political cooperation, to a second stage in which economic objectives are becoming predominant.

During the decade of ASEAN's existence, the political leaders of the region have considered the intergovernmental association primarily a mechanism for realizing political ends, particularly stability in the face of an external threat to the region. Outsiders perceived it as an anti-Communist bloc of countries committed to the West and the capitalistic model of development. Its national leaders have largely succeeded in overcoming the legacy of colonialism that politically and culturally separated their states from each other. Effective consultative processes have been established and a flurry of conferences, seminars, and resolutions has vastly increased the amount of mutual contact within the region. ASEAN's major achievement has been to create a growing awareness of regional interests. In terms of essentials, economic progress until now has been limited to the discussion of issues, as no country has been willing to transfer power to a supranational agency or to risk national interests for the possibility of regional benefits.

As Castro states, three mechanisms of economic cooperation were discussed at Bali--selective trade liberalization, industrial complementarity agreements, and package deals for investments projects. The governments decided to move forward with the allocation of regional industries, known as the package deal, and the economic ministers, meeting several months later in Kuala Lumpur, worked out the terms for the establishment of five industries in the member countries.

Castro is cautiously hopeful that progress in economic cooperation will continue and strengthen ASEAN's influence on the global economy. The likelihood of this occurring depends on economic conditions in the industrialized countries, particularly Japan and the United States, and whether potential antagonism between ASEAN and the Communist states of the region can be contained. These two conditions require consideration before attempting to assess the region's future economic influence.

As Paauw emphasizes, a dynamic foreign trade sector is a prerequisite for growth in the small, outward-looking market economies of ASEAN. Japan is the principal external influence for the following reasons:

1. The enormous size of the Japanese economy--with about 8 per cent of world gross national product, Japan follows the United States as the second largest market economy. Herman Kahn, in The Emerging Japanese Superstate, predicted that the Japanese per capita income would overtake the United States by 1985. His prediction was based on an assumed 15 per cent annual growth rate. Recent shocks to the world economy make this prediction unlikely (Japan's GNP growth rate was negative in 1974), and Japan is now growing at about 6 per cent. Whether the Japanese economy operates closer to the present 5-6 per cent rate or the pre-1973 rate of about 10 per cent will have tremendous effect upon future growth rates of the ASEAN countries.

2. Japan's aggressive trade and investment policies--in contrast to the United States, Japanese businesses have been particularly effective in integrating trade, investment, and aid objectives in individual ASEAN countries.[7] Assisted by large trading firms, the Japanese have invested in small import-substitution industries, thus shifting import requirements from Japanese finished products to Japanese intermediate goods. The pressures upon Japan to invest in the ASEAN bloc continue as

---

[7] For example see Seiji Naya and Narongchai Akrasanee, Thailand's International Economic Relations with Japan and the U.S.: A Study of Trade and Investment Interactions, Faculty of Economics Discussion Paper No. 47 (Bangkok: Thammasat University, 1975).

rising wage rates and environmental concerns encourage the export of labor-intensive and dirty industries out of Japan. Except for the Philippines and the oil sector of the Indonesian economy, the Japanese are the major investors in the ASEAN countries.

3. The natural interdependence between Japan and the ASEAN region--ASEAN's share of Japanese trade is second only to the United States. Japan depends upon imports for 95 per cent of its energy requirements, 50 per cent of its food, and the bulk of the raw materials required by its industry. The open economies of the ASEAN region depend upon Japan as a market for primary product exports and as a source of technology and industrial imports.

If the Japanese economy expands vigorously over the next decade it will have tremendous power to pull up the ASEAN economies with it. The pressure of Japanese investment would increase, both for primary product expansion and for the production of labor-intensive goods for re-export to Japan and other industrial economies. After Tanaka's disastrous visit to the ASEAN region in 1974, the Japanese are increasingly concerned about local sensitivities toward their activities, and they might be able to expand investment without triggering nationalistic backlashes. In such a dynamic situation, ASEAN could play a useful role as a multilateral negotiating mechanism for the member countries. Individual countries find their bargaining power weak in bilateral negotiations with Japan. In a context of interregional trade, the association could control the location of Japanese investment projects so their effect would be complementary rather than competitive as at present.

The Communist victory in Indochina in 1975 left the region divided between the Communist and non-Communist states. Vietnam is clearly the dominant political question mark in Southeast Asia today. Its military strength, both quantitatively and qualitatively, exceeds that of the rest of the region as a whole. Many believe that it has the potential for developing rapidly into the paramount power in the region--its regional hegemony disputed only by Indonesia. Its support of insurgency in Thailand and aggressive anti-capitalist rhetoric remind the Thais of the historic antagonism between the two nations, and they and others in ASEAN are uneasy about Vietnam's intentions in the region.

On the other hand, there are hopeful signs that the danger of a Soviet-backed political/military offensive by Vietnam in the region is declining. Hanoi's present emphasis is upon domestic reconstruction and consolidation. It has rejected the radical Chinese model of self-sufficient development and is seeking foreign aid from East and West in order to build its industrial capacity. Although its strategy has resemblances to the Soviet model, the diversification of external assistance and investment reduces reliance upon the Soviet Union itself. Hanoi states that its foreign policy is based upon a policy of mutual respect for territorial integrity and non-interference in the affairs of other nation states.

Although its population is highly disciplined and its military equipped and prepared, Vietnam is a small, poor country in the context of Southeast Asia (see Table 1). Belligerent behavior toward its ASEAN neighbors would risk jeopardizing assistance from the Western industrial states and the international agencies that it deems desirable to achieve economic goals.

While deepening political polarization between the two groups is not occurring, at least for the present, the alternative prospect of a merger of Indochina into the ASEAN group is not immediately likely either. Although such broadening of membership is an official long-term ASEAN objective, it is improbable that the fragile progress toward economic cooperation could survive a merger of such dissimilar economies. A more comprehensive political association may eventually transpire, but one likely cost would be the suspension of ASEAN's present progress toward economic cooperation. Since ASEAN was originally established for political purposes, the member nations might be willing to sacrifice the association for broader political accords within the region, particularly if present momentum in the economic sphere does not appear to be providing tangible benefits.

As a consequence of their membership in the Third World, one might expect that the two blocs could be drawn together by their common interest in establishing the New International Economic Order (NIEO) demanded by spokesmen for the LDCs. The North-South problem would then replace the East-West problem. While superficially plausible, the ASEAN nations would realize only modest benefits from the measures advocated for the NIEO. They are committed to a global economy directed by market forces that appear to have benefited them in the past. They generally reject the radical diagnosis that fundamental restructuring is required to overcome inherent defects in the system. Although both blocs participate in the Group of 77, the limits of ASEAN's substantive interest in the objectives of the NIEO make this an unlikely basis for regional association.

Politically the region is in a state of great fluidity, with tensions remaining high and the possibility of profound shifts in relationships. Favorable economic development depends directly on peace and political stability in the region. Although the prospects for a regional balance of power, with growing economic strength in both the ASEAN and the Communist groups, appear encouraging at present, the possibility of serious and sudden disruption will continue for some time.

In conclusion we return to the question addressed by the panel--Is Southeast Asia an emerging center of economic influence? An answer is suggested by a recent advertisement for the new Asian Wall Street Journal published in Hong Kong:

> . . . Asian economic growth is spectacular. (From) 1969-1974 the GNP of nine East Asian countries grew at a rate nearly triple that of the world's industrialized nations--and almost four times that of the U.S. and this is real GNP growth--after eliminating inflation's effects: Examples of GNP growth: The Philippines +34%; Thailand +37%; Japan +40%; Malaysia +41%; Indonesia +42%; Hong Kong +58%; South Korea +58%; Singapore +72%; Taiwan +143%. Today, trade between Asia and the U.S. exceeds that between the U.S. and the entire European Economic Community.[8]

This is not simple journalistic hyperbole. High growth rates have generally been regained in the ASEAN countries, as each has concentrated primarily on its internal problems of political and economic development. Although very poor by any absolute standard, the ASEAN countries have higher per capita incomes and growth rates on the average than the rest of Asia or the Third World. There are reasons for optimism that the ASEAN countries will retain this favorable position:

1. The region is relatively well endowed with social overhead facilities, private commercial services such as banking and transportation, and trained manpower. Singapore, the world's third busiest port, is centrally situated so as to be able to serve the critical foreign trade sector of the region.

2. ASEAN's progress toward economic cooperation has been halting but creditable given the deep disputes that have historically divided the region.

3. The region is large enough to permit substantial economies of scale in future industrial expansion--regional population exceeds that of the United States or the European Economic Community.

4. Assuming world demand for primary products can be sustained at a high level, foreign trade should continue to be a leading sector for the small, open ASEAN economies. The national resource base is adequate for the expansion of timber, rubber, various minerals, food grains, and other agricultural products. A buoyant world economy would then permit the ASEAN group to continue to escape the chronic balance of payments problems that plague most of the Third World.

---

[8] Quoted in G. J. Viksnins, "Pacific Asia and the New International Economic Order," (mimeographed, undated), p. 19.

Southeast Asia's economic significance both now and in the future will be low compared to the economic superpowers. But within the Third World context, it is comparable to a number of economic centers of secondary importance. Its gross product is about that of India or almost the size of Black Africa. Its economic future will be affected by the geopolitical significance of its location. It is hoped that external interests can be channeled into constructive development efforts. The high rates of economic growth that are possible in the region should increase the prospects for internal political stability. Even if the region is fortunate enough to play out this optimistic scenario for the future, it will continue as a secondary although dynamic center of economic influence and will only slowly ameliorate the poverty that impairs the quality of life in all of the Third World.

RESOURCES FOR DEVELOPMENT AND DEVELOPMENT OF RESOURCES IN SOUTHEAST ASIA

James Osborn

This paper considers the four major populous resource producing and exporting countries in Southeast Asia: Thailand, Malaysia, Indonesia, and the Philippines. It looks at the similarities and differences in the relationship of resources, especially mineral resources, to national development in the 1970s and provides an overview of current problems and prospects in the development of key resources.

RESOURCES AND DEVELOPMENT

The objectives of development policy in the 1970s for all these countries are similar: economic growth with reduction in population increases, and redistribution of the benefits of growth towards the low income segments of the population and the low income regions of the countries. Growth is to be achieved by capital investment fueled by export earnings and domestic savings and enhanced by capital transfers from the international investment and assistance systems. Export revenues and incoming investment and assistance are dependent on a degree of internal stability, both social and economic, which all of these countries have had and can be expected to retain in the 1970s. But external instability in commodity prices and the capital market, and the general world recession and inflation, are continuing problems.

In Gross National Product terms, the economies of the four countries have been growing impressively so far in the 1970s. Large increases in GNP and GNP *per capita* at current prices, ranging from 25 per cent per year from 1972/3 to 1974/5 in Thailand to 58 per cent in Indonesia, have been severely cut into by inflation which by 1973 was in double digit figures in all countries (33 per cent in Indonesia in FY 1974). But real growth and growth *per capita* have been far from stagnant. Continuing real growth in the range of three to six per cent is predicted in the current year.

The importance of resources should not be overstated. Shares in Gross Domestic Product contributed by the mining and quarrying sector remain small in all these countries. Even Indonesia had only doubled its mining share from 4.7 per cent to 9.3 per cent from 1969 to 1973. But, put another way, corporate tax on oil will account for almost 13 per cent of non-oil GDP in 1975/6, up from 4.5

per cent in 1972/3, according to the World Bank. The Philippines increased the mining share from 1.8 per cent to 2.9 per cent in the same period; Thailand's remained constant at 1.9 per cent from 1969 to 1974; and Malaysia's mining share of GDP dropped from 5.6 to 5.0 per cent in those five years.

Agriculture remains the largest contributing sector in the four countries. Its share increased to 38 per cent in Thailand in 1973, remained constant at about 36.5 per cent in the Philippines, and declined in Malaysia from a third to 24 per cent by 1974 and from 49 per cent in Indonesia in 1969 to 40 per cent in 1973. Employment in the mining sector is one half or less of a per cent of total employment in all countries except Malaysia, where in 1970 it was 2.2 per cent. Agricultural employment in 1970 ranged from 50 per cent in Malaysia to 74 per cent and 79 per cent in Indonesia and Thailand respectively.[1]

Resources are important chiefly as exports. Expenditures on Gross Domestic Product in the export sector have been growing in all countries. They are 40 per cent in Malaysia and 20 per cent or a little less in the other three countries. While Malaysia has a small but rising content of manufactured goods among its exports, Thailand, Indonesia, and the Philippines must concentrate on primary products, at least in the absence of a common economic and marketing agreement in the region. Exports, of course, are important in two ways. They permit importation of goods required for development and, in the case of Java, survival. Sustained growth as planned by the governments cannot proceed in these countries without increasing exports and maintaining a reasonable balance of trade. This is an increasingly tense issue as general inflation in the West and the large oil price rise have vastly enlarged import bills for manufactured products as well as crude oil.

The second way in which exports are important is as a direct source of revenue to governments. Although all of these countries have modified free-enterprise economies, the public sector, or state capitalism, is becoming increasingly significant. It is dominant in Indonesia, involves more than 50 per cent of the total planned capital investment this year in Malaysia, and is developing in the forms of state mining and other resource development and utility enterprises, if not

---

[1] Figures are from official sources for all national aggregates and breakdowns unless otherwise noted. They are to be treated with the customary caution. See tables in Appendix B.

manufacturing, in Thailand and the Philippines. Furthermore, the greatest single force for change in these countries is the central government--by regulation and especially by budget expenditures on projects, by transfers to local governments, and the deployment of foreign loans they guarantee. All countries have gone increasingly to both domestic and foreign borrowing in recent years to finance development. There is little doubt that the stability and growth or growth potential (in Thailand's case) in the commodities export business is an important element in the credit worthiness of these countries and their governments.

Except in the case of Indonesia, government revenues derived from resources industries are small but rising. The success of development plans depends on their growth. Thailand's revenue from exports in 1975 was only five per cent of total revenues, $108 million, to which rice exports contributed 57 per cent. In 1974, Malaysian tax revenue from exports was $113 million, or 7.6 per cent of total revenues. Tin contributed $42 million and rubber $34 million. In 1972/3 the Philippines export tax revenue was a mere 6.6 per cent of total tax revenue, although in 1973 and most of 1974 the government was able to derive extra revenues from copper exports during the copper boom through a premium in addition to the export tax. Indonesia, of course, is the purest case of mineral export benefit to government revenues. In 1975/6 petroleum royalties contributed 63.3 per cent of tax revenues and 56.5 per cent of total planned expenditures.

In all countries annual spending by central governments on development has increased dramatically in the 1970s, although the impact of this spending has been reduced by high inflation. In current terms, Thailand's development budget almost doubled between 1969 and 1972/3, Malaysia's more than doubled between 1969 and 1974, Indonesia's increased 12 times between 1970/1 and 1976/7, and that of the Philippines more than doubled between 1969/70 and 1972/3.

Owing to the heavy overseas investment content in resource development in these countries, the governmental capital or development expenditure in mining or industry and in mining categories is also quite small compared to that in agriculture, communications and transportation, and even education. It is not significantly rising in any of these countries but Malaysia, where industrial development, though not really mining as yet, has become more important since the late sixties. There, expenditures on mining and industry rose to 16 per cent of the 1974 development budget, up from 6.6 per cent in 1969. In Thailand the proportion dropped from one to one half of a per cent by 1975. In Indonesia the proportion rose from two to three per cent between 1970/1 and 1975/6, while in the Philippines it declined from two to 0.1 per cent between 1969/70 and 1972/3.

The exports of all countries, expressed in current prices, increased dramatically in the first half of the 1970s. They more than doubled in dollar value in Thailand and Malaysia (in Malaysia the US dollar lost value relative to the Malaysian dollar, however), tripled in the Philippines and quadrupled in Indonesia. The principal exports were all natural resource products and went mostly to Japan. Imports kept pace and, even with net capital movement considered, caused balance of payment deficits by 1975 in all but Malaysia, which has the highest developed import substitution industrialization. Indonesia's net oil exports rose from 21 per cent of the value of total exports in 1971/2 to an estimated 61 per cent in 1975/6. The balance of payments is deteriorating in all countries.

There is considerable, but, of course, far from complete similarity in the commodity composition of exports of these four countries. Thailand, Malaysia, and Indonesia export rubber and tin in quantity. While the value of exports in these commodities has increased between 1969 and 1974 for all three countries, almost doubling in the case of Thailand, and more than doubling in the other two, the ratios of these export earnings to total export receipts has declined between 25 and 50 per cent. Price instability is one factor. More important has been the increasing importance of other exports. Thailand's rubber and tin exports fell from 19 per cent and 11.5 per cent of total export values in 1969, to ten per cent and six per cent respectively. Sugar and tapioca exports increased but the proportion of commodities exports to total exports declined from 79 per cent to 67 per cent. Malaysian rubber and tin exports, as proportions of total export values, fell from 40.7 per cent and 18.8 per cent, respectively, to 30 per cent and 14.6 per cent. Palm oil exports increased from three to 11 per cent of exports by 1974, petroleum and petroleum products from three to seven per cent. Palm oil is projected to have been the top export in 1975 ($M293 mil versus $M178 mil for tin and $M109 mil from rubber), despite a price decline from 1971 to 1976 of 40 per cent.[2] Primary products as a proportion of total exports fell between 1969 and 1974 from 89 to 79 per cent in Malaysia.

In Indonesia, petroleum exports have now overshadowed all others, due almost entirely to the price rises. As in Thailand and Malaysia, export values of rubber, tin, palm oil, and forest products have continued to rise since 1969, by a factor

---

[2] *Far Eastern Economic Review*, 19 December 1975, p. 53.

of two in rubber, almost four in tin and almost 29 for forest products. In FY74 timber was the highest income earner after oil ($631 mil). The Philippines' large resources and resource products exports are sugar, copper, coconut oil, forest products, and copra. Sugar is the highest valued. It advanced from 18.4 per cent of total exports by value in 1969 to 38.8 per cent in 1974, and increased in value 4.68 times. Copper increased its share in the same period from 15.5 per cent to 20.6 per cent, and its value 2.95 times. In this period exports of copra and forest products stagnated. But price drops through 1975 could mean a decline in copper earnings of as much as 25 per cent over 1973 and early 1974.[3]

Exports in current values are projected by various authorities to continue to rise in all these commodities in all countries in the next year and probably through the 1970s, despite the waning of the world wide commodity boom in 1974. (That year the tin market, for example, weakened by 31 per cent.) But the historic decline in real prices for commodities is said to be "a strong but not wholly conclusive reason to suppose that no general [price] rise will occur" soon; while generally, "an underlying tendency to wide price fluctuations can be anticipated for the primary commodities."[4] From 1970 to 1973 the rise in commodity prices, for example, was considerably higher than increases in imported manufactured goods world wide. But in 1974 the terms of trade deteriorated. Malaysia's decline in terms of trade is expected to eliminate the traditional merchandise account surplus in the near future.[5]

We see that increasing primary product exports is most important to growth in Indonesia, and least important in Malaysia which, incidentally, are the two countries with the finest mineral and mineral fuel endowments and prospects. Thailand and the Philippines must continue to strive for increased exports and export diversification to overcome balance of payment problems and market effects and to guarantee the continued inflow of loans and investments. Only Indonesia can be said to be dependent on mineral resource exports for its viability. Malaysia has successfully diversified its export sector far beyond the point possible to the other countries in this decade. And this promises to support in that country its growing standard of living, which is already more than twice as high as that in Thailand and the Philippines, and almost four times Indonesia's, based on GDP *per capita* calculations. Current

---

[3] FEER, (fn. 2), 4 April 1975, p. 54.

[4] *Trade in Primary Commodities: Conflict on Cooperation?* A Tripartite Report by Fifteen Economists (Washington: Brookings, 1974), pp. 24-5.

[5] FEER, (fn. 2), 29 April 1975, p. 10.

hopes for urban industrial development, of course, face severe domestic market limitations, among other imponderables, in all four countries.

Thus the importance of resources to development is limited. Their exploitation touches directly only a small proportion of the population. The countries' national product and government revenues for development, excepting the oil and gas industries in Indonesia, are not overwhelmed by the primary products export sector. Yet the support of overall development that such exports and their increase provide to these governments is certainly crucial, especially in times of inflation and energy crises in the developed countries. Hla Myint, in a major policy review of the economy of Southeast Asia in the 1970s, prescribed a policy of maximization of benefits from trade in natural resources, particularly minerals, mineral fuels and timber.[6] This recommendation has been heeded. The question now is: what are the problems and prospects for development of key resources in these countries?

DEVELOPMENT OF RESOURCES

The problems in mineral resource development are (a) provision of sufficient investment for exploration and production, (b) conflicts over profitability between the countries and the international companies involved, (c) price fluctuations on the international market, (d) depletion, and (e) in the case of oil for export, competition with increasing domestic use. Profit from mineral product exports can be increased by additional processing, mainly refining, prior to export. This policy goal is gradually being achieved for mineral resources other than crude oil. Mineral products do not have some of the disadvantages which agricultural and silvicultural exports share. For example, minerals can be stored easily, although in some cases expensively. Their production can be cut back readily when prices drop. And the ones important in Southeast Asia are not threatened by substitution in the middle-run under current and foreseeable price conditions. Their development does not imply complex organization of manpower and disruption of traditional patterns (except mainland onshore tin). And in most cases large integrated international corporations are available to handle the actual mineral exploitation and sales.

None of the usual problems of mineral resource development appear to be especially important in the four countries under consideration for the next two decades. Led by Indonesia and Malaysia, these countries have mostly resolved the issues of

---

[6] _Southeast Asia's Economy: Development Policies in the 1970's_, a study sponsored by the Asian Development Bank (New York: Praeger, 1972), pp. 75, 102.

creating mechanisms for satisfactory bargaining between governments and companies over profit sharing. Thailand is the least advanced in this, having had crises in offshore tin mining and up-country zinc refining investment that have shut down several operations, presumably temporarily. Depletion of old mining sites has, in almost all cases, been balanced by new discoveries and, in the case of tin, the possibilities of new extractive technologies. The upward swing in the economy of the developed countries suggests not only continued and increasing demand for most minerals, but adequate availability of investment capital. All four countries, furthermore, are believed to have commercially exploitable quantities of minerals, both new and traditional, which are as yet untapped. There is no prospect, however, for an OPEC effect on the prices of mineral exports from these countries other than oil and gas, whose earnings are expected to steadily increase to 1990.

Thus, generally speaking, the prospects are good for a continued and important contribution from mineral development to national development in the next twenty years. After that most known important deposits will be depleted, if present and contemplated rates of production continue. Further discoveries cannot be predicted now. The real problems of resources, therefore, are not their development and profitability, supposing the world and local economies meet no disaster, but consist in putting their export earnings to work solving other economic and social problems, including preparation for the time when mineral resource exports fall off.

At this time, this apparently does not call for decreasing dependence on the export sector, but rather for hastened development of renewable product exports. Timber, rubber, palm and coconut oil, and sugar, in addition to rice in Thailand, offer the best possibilities. Unfortunately, the organizational, if not investment problems associated with such development are considerably more difficult than those already surmounted with minerals and mineral fuels. Palm oil and sugar have the better export market potential, with rubber holding its own. Eventually employment will be the biggest problem in these countries, possibly excluding Malaysia. Resource development of any sort cannot be expected to contribute to the solution of this problem, except, as is the present case, by paying for imports and guaranteeing external loans through the end of the century.

Oil and Gas

Until very recently, Indonesia has been the only country under consideration here with significant oil and gas production. Oil production rose from 312 million barrels in 1970 to 515 in 1974, with older fields falling off and newer ones coming on stream. Malaysia's oil production actually declined slightly from 34 to 32.6 million barrels between 1972 and 1975. Marketed natural gas rose more slowly in Indonesia, but increased in Malaysia by about a third in the period to roughly one seventeenth of Indonesia's. Indonesia's oil production is increasing unsteadily, with production down to 1.2 million barrels a day in June 1975 from 1.5 million in 1974, but topping 1.5 million barrels per day in March 1976 and averaging 1.51 in August. Pertamina, the Indonesian national oil company, has the goal of three million barrels per day by 1980, which is realistic even considering the company's current reorganization and cash flow problems. Malaysia, on the other hand, appears headed for a dramatic increase in oil and natural gas production from fields in Sabah, with export values expected to have increased by 50 per cent in 1975 and another 50 per cent in 1976. Daily production of crude is expected to reach 200,000 barrels in 1977 and could be double that by 1980, with 80 per cent or more exported.[7]

Thailand and the Philippines produced negligible amounts of gas and oil through 1975. In 1976 the Philippines announced that oil was beginning to flow from a well 30 miles northwest of Palawan. Thai offshore explorations have not been promising thus far; although there are prospects for gas production piped to Bangkok to eliminate the need for energy imports in the electric power industry.

Indonesia has led in innovative petroleum development. A crucial element is generous terms to international companies, either via production sharing with or contract to Pertamina, to explore for oil and gas. These carry the implication of further company cooperation in production and a monopoly on international marketing. Pertamina retains complete control of domestic marketing and seeks to increase its share in the processing of oil and gas for export, financing this by international borrowing. Pertamina at the same time takes responsibility for servicing the foreign companies whose technology and skilled manpower it cannot duplicate. It makes them comfortable in degrees beyond those attainable by other foreign companies in the economy. As production success increases and, at least, while petroleum products are in a sellers market, Indonesia improves the terms by which it shares the benefits, although there is current resistance to more of this from the foreign companies, especially Caltex, the largest producer. And the international oil

---

[7] Economist Intelligence Unit, Malaysia-Singapore-Brunei, No. 1 (February 1975), p. 8. Current adjustments in oil policy have led to a reduction in the estimate of 1980 production to 250,000 barrels per day from the earlier 400,000 barrels per day. See FEER, (fn. 2), 27 August 1976, p. 54.

industry claims that increasing the production sharing ratios much further in favor of the countries will curtail new exploration dramatically. This remains to be seen.

Until late 1975 Pertamina was an autonomous entity, though state owned. This probably improved efficiency, but it weakened the grasp of the Ministry of Finance on the enormous profits and of the economic planners on its adventurism. Included in the more than three billion dollars worth of short term company debts and the US $10 billion overall financial crisis worrying everyone in June 1975 were $850 million owed to the government itself. The Ministry of Finance is now in control. But as a result the company has dropped non-oil sector development plans as well as plans to construct three large export-oriented refineries in Batam Island near Singapore.

Indonesia has had the most comprehensive oil search in Asia. It covered almost all the shelf areas and, including mineral exploration, 30 per cent of the land area by 1974.[8] In 1974 alone, 231 exploratory wells were drilled, yielding 28 oil, 25 gas and oil and 18 gas strikes. Foreign contractors invested more than $700 million in exploration and development between 1968 and 1973, followed by a geometrical rise through 1975, when foreign, mainly US, contractors planned a record $1,200 million investment. That is about ten times as much as investment in other fields. Japanese banks in 1975 pledged investment of over one billion dollars for gas development.[9]

A major Indonesian problem is increasing domestic consumption of oil. The domestic fuel allocation applied to oil producing companies increased from 15.4 per cent in 1974 to 17.9 per cent in 1975 and 19.6 per cent already in 1976. Domestic consumption is expected to increase by 13 per cent per year. Ibnu Sutowo, former President-Director of Pertamina, when in command, stated that, "if the economic goals of the Southeast Asian nations are achieved, the region will be in a deficit energy resource position." Domestic sales of oil are relatively unprofitable to foreign oil companies. In fact the present arrangements constitute a somewhat hidden tax benefit to the government. Thus, increasing domestic consumption supported by government imposed allocations, in addition to reduced profits on

---

[8] See ECAFE, Regional Conference on Geology and Mineral Resources Development, Draft Report (October 1973); and M. Semay, "Oil and Mineral Developments," Bulletin of Indonesian Economic Statistics VIII, No. 3 (November 1972), p. 131.

[9] Far Eastern Economic Review Yearbook 1976 (Hong Kong: Far Eastern Economic Review, 1975), pp. 80-187. In August 1976, foreign oil companies and Pertamina were reported to be spending US $3 million a day in the oil search. But a trend cannot be discerned. See FEER, (fn. 2), 20 August 1976, p. 36.

foreign sales, can discourage investment in exploration. And only intensive new exploration can expand the proved reserves. In the absence of that and at current production levels, Indonesian oil will be gone in 20 years and its natural gas in 40.[10]

Malaysia is in the enviable position of having potentially important oil and gas supplies, certainly enough to cover imports and make a small contribution to the balance of payments, particularly via liquified natural gas (LNG), while being far from desperate for foreign investment and increased export sales. The historic attractiveness of Malaysia to resource exploiting foreign companies, however, has met with the lessons Malaysia has learned from Indonesia. The Malaysian government moved hesitantly but established *Petronas*, the national petroleum development and marketing company, in 1975. It is backed with tough legislation which, *inter alia*, would appear to permit it effortlessly to acquire control, though not ownership, of a foreign company in the production, refining, or marketing business. Initial negative reaction among the oil companies resulted in cancellation of Exxon's exploration activities off West Malaysia after a $300 million investment, and shelving of plans for a Caltex refinery. Agreements which Malaysia hopes will be superior to Indonesia's are being negotiated haltingly with the companies. These are to include production sharing with Exxon on production off the East coast of Malaya and around Sabah, and, more importantly, a majority share in a planned $1,100 million LNG plant off Sarawak in cooperation with Sarawak Shell and Mitsubishi.

Thailand and the Philippines remain in the speculative stage of petroleum development. Yet their balance of payments problems are such that solid encouragement is being given to multinational companies to speed up exploration with an eye to import substitution. In the Philippines since 1972 foreigners have been urged to explore, and this is being done by the smaller oil companies. Twelve wells were planned in the North Palawan Basin in 1975 at a cost of $50 million. Onshore exploration includes eleven wells and the involvement of the Philippines National Oil Company in the Cagayan Valley of Luzon.

Thai exploration in the Gulf of Thailand was cut in half after the end of the Indo-China War and in the wake of anti-foreign investment sentiments in the post-military regime. Another problem is the unresolved boundary dispute between

---

[10] *FEER*, (fn. 2), 19 March 1976, pp. 59-60.

Thailand and Cambodia in the Gulf. Slow progress in this case cannot be blamed on too heavy emulation of Indonesia and Malaysia, as Thailand has no national oil company and has made no move so far to tighten its Petroleum Act, which is favorable towards exploration companies.[11] Natural gas is now the more promising development. As of January 1976, Union Oil estimated it had found reserves of at least one trillion cubic feet of gas in a field 100 miles out in the Gulf,[12] sufficient to supply the electricity authority of Thailand up to the level of current demand for oil. But the $500 million cost for development and the underwater pipeline could be too high, even considering that Thailand's import bill for oil was $600 million in 1974, up 160 per cent over the previous year.

Malaysia and Indonesia can expect their major LNG market to be Japan. With Brunei they have four per cent of the world's proven recoverable gas reserves, totalling about 55 trillion cubic feet. These countries also have a price advantage over potential LNG imports from the Middle East to Japan. And oil company executives are still saying that the prospects for oil and gas exploitation in Indonesia and East Malaysia are extremely promising.[13]

Immediate and middle term competition, especially for the Japanese market, however, is a concern to Indonesia and Malaysia. Indonesia's drop in oil sales to Japan of 25 per cent from 1974 to 1975 appears to have been largely the result of Chinese price competition. China beat Indonesia's OPEC-determined uniform price of $12.80 f.o.b. with a price of $12.10 per barrel for, admittedly, inferior (higher parafin content) crude. Chinese sales doubled in 1975. This meant that Japan, as a market, fell from a 71.4 per cent share of Indonesian exports (in 1973) to less than half. Indonesia countered by dropping prices slightly and by increasing exports of its highly desirable low-sulphur crude to the western United States. This largely off-set the Japanese loss.[14] With such success and normal Chinese unpredictability in mind, the FY76 Indonesian budget projects net oil income of $4 billion, a third more than that of the previous year.

Even if alternative markets to Japan continue to be open as world production

---

[11] See <u>FEER</u>, (fn. 2), 8 August 1975, p. 41.

[12] <u>FEER</u>, (fn. 2), 9 January 1976, p. 36. See also Ibid.

[13] <u>FEER</u>, (fn. 2), 20 June 1975, pp. 47-9.

[14] <u>FEER</u>, (fn. 2), 6 February 1976, p. 38; and 26 March 1976, pp. 42-3.

of oil and gas declines in the next few decades and alternative energy sources are not yet fully developed, reorienting export vectors could still be disruptive and potentially bad for Indonesia and Malaysia. China and the USSR emerge as the likely competitors in Asian and Pacific trade, and in the short run could be mischievous. One China watcher has predicted that by the mid-1980s China could be exporting over 100 million tons of oil, much of it to Japan.[15] Another suggests that by 1980 China could have equalled Indonesia's share of the Japanese oil market.[16] Likewise, the Soviet Union has promising prospects for onshore and offshore oil and gas finds at Sakhalin, not to mention Siberia, and 27.5 per cent of the world's proven gas reserves.[17]

Tin

Tin production in Thailand, Malaysia, and Indonesia contributed about 53 per cent of world production in 1973. Production has been slowly rising in Thailand and Indonesia in the 1970s and gradually falling in Malaysia. Malaysia has been producing about 30 per cent of the world's tin and the other two about ten per cent each. Thailand has the largest estimated reserves of the three (33.5 per cent of world reserves); while Malaysia and Indonesia have comparably smaller reserves (14.4 and 13.2 per cent respectively). Indonesia's goal is a ten per cent increase in production yearly, which it achieved from 1971 through 1974. Malaysia's production peaked in 1972 (at 76,808 tons or 32.5 per cent of world output) and has been declining by between four and seven per cent per year through 1975. The Malaysian government, however, feels it could expect annual production to stabilize at between 65,000 and 70,000 tons through the end of the decade.[18] Tin exported from the region is almost entirely refined metal from Malaysia (where much ore from Thailand and Indonesia is refined in addition to its own entire ore production) and from Thailand. Indonesia will put its first tin smelter into full operation on Bangka Island in 1976.

Considering the reserves positions of all these countries, exploration and

---

[15] Barry Richman, "Oil for the Lamps of America and Other Matters Chinese," Center Report IX, No. 2 (April 1976), p. 15.

[16] Ho Ping-ti, quoted in FEER Yearbook 1976, (fn. 9), p. 81.

[17] FEER, (fn. 2), 20 June 1975, p. 47.

[18] FEER, (fn. 2), 1 August 1975, p. 37.

technology are important factors in increasing production. Indonesia is exploring between its tin islands of Bangka and Belitung and throughout the whole tin islands area where it is known that commercial tin ore occurs. In 1971, 60 per cent of production came from offshore works. Malaysia's declining tin output may be reversed by discoveries in 1974 by the national mining company, Pernas, dredging 150 miles off the Perak coast and off Malacca. Known onshore deposits exist in many cases belcw the 200 feet maximum depth of current dredges, thus requiring an advance in mining technology as a precondition to exploration, as is also possibly the case for new mining in Pahang and Johore.

Thailand is believed to have large economic offshore deposits. But Thailand's tin production problem is complex compared to that of the other countries. About 75 per cent of production has been onshore, mainly Thai-owned, and utilizing comparatively primitive technology. It is believed that the future of tin mining in Thailand lies offshore. That is where three foreign-controlled companies dominate, employing sophisticated, capital-intensive techniques. In 1975 all this came to a crisis when the mining concessions of the major company, Thailand Exploration and Mining Company (TEMCO), owned mainly by Union Carbide and Royal Dutch Shell, were cancelled for legal reasons, which appear actually to be mainly political ones. Mining operations were suspended in January, after an investment of around $15 million including employment of the world's largest suction-cutter dredge. Further investment of $20 million in a third and last dredge was cancelled. A total of at least $60 million in new investment by multinationals was put in doubt with a potential loss to the Thai government of $30 million a year from the new tin that would have been mined. What all this means is a temporary slow down of growth in Thai tin production while Thailand resolves the problem of its relations with foreign investors and falls in step with Malaysia and Indonesia.[19]

Another important factor in production growth is price. As prices rise and fall on the international market, mining operations open and close, affecting output, especially in Malaysia. The problem is exacerbated by the rising costs of tin mining. Gravel pump mining costs per unit rose 52 per cent between 1973 and 1975. In 1974 the tin price hit a record of $M1,380 a picul (113.3 lbs. to a picul), falling back to a little more than $M900 at the beginning of 1976, which is about the cost of production in the more expensive operations. In the first eight months of 1975 the

---

[19] See FEER, (fn. 2), 4 April 1976, pp. 36-7.

number of active tin mines in Malaysia fell accordingly from 1,025 to 960.[20]

The floor price of tin established by the International Tin Council (ITC) is also $M900 per picul. ITC is a comparatively successful price control mechanism, partly because it consists of consuming as well as producing nations, and partly because price stabilization, in both directions, is so critical, especially the floor for the producers. Substantial increases in tin prices in the near future, it is believed, could not be maintained because of competition from aluminum, tin-free steel, and plastics in some of the major tin uses.[21] A floor price is necessary, as we have seen, because of the price effect on production in an inflationary period. In June 1975, the Fifth Tin Agreement was signed, imposing slightly higher price limits for five years beginning in July of 1976. It seeks to stabilize prices by the use of both buffer stocks and export control measures and, *inter alia*, doubles buffer stocks to 40,000 tons through voluntary contributions. The old agreement appeared to be effective during the latter half of 1974 when, as prices fell towards $M900 per picul, additional buffer stock contributions and export controls were called for and the price slide was halted.

The problem with the ITC is that although its membership has been enlarged to seven producing countries and 22 consuming countries, China and Brazil, both growing producers, and the United States, the largest consumer are not members. The United States has made major interventions in the tin market from its stockpiles over the years. From 1970 to 1973, for example, it released 4,500 long tons, average, per year, and in June 1974, 23,542 long tons. This upset Malaysia extremely. However the United States appears now to be on the verge of joining the Council. In the long run this ought to cause slightly higher world prices and thereby perhaps more investment.[22] Japan was hesitant about participation in 1975, seemingly more from a concern about precedent and immediate costs of contributions than an implicit tendency to slight price rises. China, meanwhile, has been increasing tin exports. In 1975 China's sales were equivalent to about 23 per cent of Malaysia's production. Peking has yet to be persuaded to join the ITC and has contributed to the 9,000 ton

---

[20] *FEER*, (fn. 2), 2 January 1976, p. 37.

[21] E. Stern and Wouter Tims, "The Relative Bargaining Strengths of the Developing Countries," in *Changing Resource Problems of the Fourth World*, ed., Ronald Ridker (Washington: Resources for the Future, 1976), pp. 29, 42.

[22] See International Economic Studies Institute, *Basic Data for Estimating U.S. Mineral Requirements and Availability* (Washington: 1976), pp. 93-4.

surplus in the world tin market of January 1976.[23] Such a large factor as China's increasing export promotion could upset the delicate balances in pricing, stockpiling, and internal taxation and compensation that is essential to the tin industry in Southeast Asia. The foreign policy contradictions for China are interesting.

Other Minerals

All four countries under consideration have other mineral deposits. Production and incoming investment that are important to them are not sources of major problems except in the case of zinc smelting in Thailand. The region is certainly mineral resource rich and varied. With the exception of copper, which is the Philippines' second largest export after sugar, none of these minerals has the potential to affect balance of payments or national income growth significantly. With respect to the various other minerals only the Philippines and Thailand among the four countries rank high as world producers (the Philippines eighth in copper, and sixth in chromite, Thailand third in tungsten). And none of these minerals, including copper but probably excepting bauxite (which, in world terms is inconsequential in Southeast Asia) has a world market situation that would seem to permit cartel or even ITC style arrangements. Yet markets generally appear to call for continued expansion, and internal conditions, even in Thailand, continue to justify international investment.

Copper production has been steadily increasing in the Philippines in the 1970s. But activity slowed as the bottom fell out of the price in early 1974, causing a probable loss of as much as $125 million in export earnings in 1975. The Philippines has kept up production and exports despite the cutbacks by the larger exporters, arguing that her exports are minimal in world trade and dependent on Japanese good will. Two worrisome current problems are cutbacks in Japan's purchases owing to the recession, and the increasing cost of production relative to prices. Nevertheless, the major producer companies are proceeding, though cautiously, with expansion of production and smelting, even as the government has abolished the mining depletion allowance (formerly 50 per cent of gross revenue), replacing it with a much less attractive 120 per cent write-off of development costs. This follows from the fact that the mining industry was the most profitable component of the industrial sector in both 1973 and 1974.[24]

---

[23] FEER, (fn. 2), 2 January 1976, p. 37.

[24] FEER, (fn. 2), 1 August 1975, p. 36.

The greatest expansion is by Atlas Consolidated, which already operates the largest open pit copper mines in the region. Existing daily capacity of 70,000 tons will be increased by almost one third at a cost of about $100 million. Atlas, however, has deferred plans to build a $235 million copper smelter, apparently because the government insisted on Cebu as the site. The company's desired one, near metro-Manila power sources, was unacceptable according to industrial development policy favoring dispersal of industry. Another company is being encouraged by the government to build a smelter in the central Philippines, but near a power supply. Known copper reserves in the Philippines are 1,859 million tons. There are good possibilities for new discoveries to maintain, if not drastically increase, production in the next two decades.

Indonesia and Sabah (Malaysia) are entering the copper export market. West Irian's production, following an investment of about $140 million by Freeport Indonesia, should achieve exports of 58,500 tons (ore content) annually, about one quarter that of the Philippines, and with an export value of $60 million.[25] The Mamut copper mine in Sabah has also begun operations. Malaysia expects a yearly output of 30,000 tons of copper ore per year.

The two most interesting mineral development departures in the region are resumed <u>coal</u> development and new bauxite smelting, both in Sumatra. Indonesia's oldest coal workings in South Sumatra are believed to constitute one of the largest recoverable low-sulphur coal deposits in the world. The international energy market has made these economical again and so Batubara, the Indonesian national coal company, signed a contract in October 1975 with Shell Mijnbouw for exploitation. In recent years Indonesian coal production has been negligible (less than 160,000 tons in 1974). This new development calls for investment of $1.2 billion on a 71,480 square kilometer concession and annual production by 1981, at 70 per cent of planned capacity, of 30 million tons. Entirely for export, coal from this development is expected to yield as much as $500 million per year at peak output. Coal would thus become the second largest foreign exchange earner for Indonesia, almost three times as great as tin.[26] There is something dubious about all this, not least concerning the organizational problems, but it is a delightful possibility. Coal production

---

[25] Semay, "Oil and Mineral . . .", (fn. 8), p. 140.

[26] See <u>FEER</u>, (fn. 2), 14 November 1975, pp. 36-7; and <u>FEER Yearbook 1976</u>, (fn. 9), p. 14.

is low and declining in Thailand. It is low but increasing (up 30 per cent in 1974 over 1973 with a threefold increase in export earnings) in the Philippines.

Bauxite exports from Indonesia to Japan have been steady at around 1.2 million tons, a little more than Malaysia exports. It is the development of a large smelter in association with the Asahan hydro-power scheme in North Sumatra that is particularly important to Indonesia. The agreement on this was finally signed in July 1975 between the Indonesian government and a Japanese consortium. This calls for a capital investment of at least $830 million, to include $300 million for the aluminum refinery which is supposed to reach full production of 225,000 tons of aluminum per year by 1983. The powerplant will have a generating capacity of 480,000 kilowatts and, with the shear enormity of the construction task, is regarded as the motive force for general development in the region. Smelting of alumina and aluminum smelting investment are also contemplated in southern Mindanao and Leyte in the Philippines, the latter employing geothermal power.

Significant nickle deposits exist in Eastern Indonesia and the Philippines (Mindanao and Luzon). Production has been increasing slowly but investment in mining and refining is picking up. A US-Dutch consortium is considering an investment of up to $1 billion on Indonesia's Gag Island (off West Irian) to develop known nickle deposits. New export earnings are expected to be $180 million annually. Mines and a smelter have been developed in Central Sulawesi at a cost of over $135 million and deposits are being developed elsewhere.[27] In the Philippines the Marinduque Mining Company began shipping nickle from its new $270 million refinery in Mindanao, ASEAN's first, in April 1975. This has become, for the Philippines, a major mineral industry. It is expected to bring in an additional $100 million in export earnings annually.[28]

Chromite is a steady but undynamic mineral industry in the Philippines, earning $11 million in 1974. This is pretty much the case also with iron and gold; although higher gold earnings (it is currently the country's third most important metal) and greater recovery have resulted from the gold price rise and because most production is a by-product of copper mining.[29]

[27] U.S. Bureau of Mines, "Indonesia," in Minerals Yearbook 1973 Vol. III (Washington: 1975), p. 8.

[28] FEER, (fn. 2), 1 August 1975, p. 37.

[29] FEER, (fn. 2), 13 June 1975, p. 15.

Zinc, _fluorite_, _manganese_, _tungsten_, _lead_ and _gypsum_ are mineral products of some importance to Thailand, but not the other countries, with the partial exception of manganese in Indonesia and the Philippines. Fluorite production, like that of tin, has stabilized in Thailand, while tungsten and manganese have fluctuated on a slow rise so far in the 1970s. Thailand was the world's third largest producer of tungsten between 1971 and 1973 (about 4,000 tons per year behind the Soviet Union and China) and the world's leading tungsten exporter in those years.[30] Zinc production tripled between 1970 and 1973. But Southeast Asia's first zinc smelter, to cost $90 million and smelt 50,000 tons of ore per year, has, as noted above, had its plans suspended. The reason in this case is disagreements between the company and the government over continued exportation of ore. The discovery in northeast Thailand of _potash_ in commercial quantities may signal export opportunities for Thailand as the region's only exporter of potash fertilizers.[31] _Gold_, _mercury_, _titanium_ and _lead_ are reported to exist in commercially viable amounts in central Malaya.[32]

Agricultural and Silvicultural Resources

Rubber production in Malaysia, Thailand, and Indonesia has been fairly constant in the 1970s. Indonesia's production has increased, with growing exports due in part to the country's non-cooperation with the Association of Natural Rubber Producing Countries (ANRPC), of which it is a member, to reduce exports as prices were falling in 1974. Malaysia and Indonesia together control more than 70 per cent of the export trade in natural rubber. Synthetic rubber produced elsewhere supplies 68 per cent of world rubber consumption; but the rise in oil prices has made natural rubber reasonably competitive with it for the foreseeable future. Thailand is the world's third largest exporter of rubber. Rubber was Thailand's second highest export revenue earner in 1973 (after rice) and third in 1974. Malaysia has the edge in technological applications and the lead in replanting over Indonesia and Thailand. It has taken the lead, as well, in controlling prices, unilaterally at times, in a manner similar to that of the ITC. And prospects for multilateral success at this seem good. There was, in fact, agreement in May 1975 among ANRPC countries to adopt a price stabilization scheme. Thus, there is a real likelihood of maintaining

---

[30] _FEER_, (fn. 2), 9 July 1976, p. 32.

[31] _FEER_, (fn. 2), 18 April 1975.

[32] _FEER_, (fn. 2), 1 August 1975, p. 37.

sufficiently high prices still fully competitive with synthetics.[33] Malaysia has ceased to arbitrarily replace rubber with oil palm for this and other reasons.

Palm Oil export prospects for the rest of the decade are fine, following the continuing strong upward price trend in food oils generally. In 1974 palm oil was the third highest export revenue earner for the Malaysian government after rubber and tin. Revised estimates for 1975 indicate that palm oil will have been that country's top revenue earner in 1975, despite a price decline beginning in 1974. It is expected to net $M293 million versus $M178 million from tin and $M109 from rubber in revenue. Oil refined locally was expected to increase 130 per cent in 1975 over 1974. Eight mills are in operation and 28 more approved for construction, all directed at export to the US.[34] Malaysia now accounts for 40% of world palm oil production and 66% of world palm oil exports.[35] Indonesian palm oil production has been expanding steadily, with export values approaching those of tin in 1974. There is serious concern, however, that at the projected rate of production expansion in these two countries and in West Africa, there will be a palm oil glut in the 1980s. Consequent lower prices could be a severe blow to Malaysia. A commodity agreement, even such as that for rubber, appears impractical owing to substitutability of other vegetable oils.

Sugar export value more than doubled in both the Philippines and Thailand between 1973 and 1974, with 20 per cent and seven per cent increases in production, respectively. Sugar production in Indonesia has failed, so far, even to keep up with domestic demand. The government is attempting to expand production in the Outer Islands.[36] By contrast, in the Philippines sugar export trade was almost twice that of copper, yet there have been recent problems of overstock. They are mitigated, if not solved by recently reported sales to Russia (400,000 tons for delivery over the next 14 months) and by the increasing purchases by Japan, which took 56 per cent of the Philippine sugar exports in 1975. The United States took

---

[33] See FAO Commodity Review and Outlook 1974-1975 (Rome: 1975), pp. 216-17.

[34] FEER, (fn. 2), 19 December 1975, pp. 51-2.

[35] FEER, (fn. 2), 9 July 1976, p. 41.

[36] See "Survey of Recent Developments," Bulletin of Indonesian Economic Statistics XI, No. 2 (July 1975), p. 21.

25 per cent, as opposed to 75 per cent the year before.[37]

The Forest Products industry in Southeast Asia is not regarded as promising growth in profits over the short run, although prices have rebounded following the extremely low price levels of 1974 and the general decline since the late 1960s. Indonesia is first in Asia and seventh in the world in area under forest, but has been restraining softwood output due to the bad market. The hardwood market remains strong, and large investments in production, though not processing, have been made. The projected rate of increase in forestry production, meaning hardwood, is eight per cent annually through 1985.[38] Sabah has an estimated 50 per cent of its land suitable for tree and food crops, with the forestry industry contributing 80 per cent of the exports of that state in 1973 (30 per cent in Sarawak). Forest products were 17.3 per cent of the value of Indonesia's exports in 1974, 13.2 per cent of Malaysia's and 12.9 per cent of the Philippines', in spite of the poor market. Philippine log and timber products exports declined precipitously from 1973 to 1975, though, (from $415 million to $150 million). Market problems there have joined recent government measures banning or heavily restricting log exports in an effort to stimulate the timber processing industry and reduce denudation.[39]

Indonesia's pepper exports more than doubled between 1969 and 1974, as did Malaysia's, with the market holding up. In each country they constituted one per cent or less of total export values. Copra exports from Indonesia, Malaysia, and the Philippines stagnated in the same period. Only in the Philippines is copra, with coconut oil, an important export. Values in the latter more than doubled in export trade between 1973 and 1974. Together in 1974 they represented about 27 per cent of export values, second to sugar and ahead of copper. There ought to be room for further development.

Rice is the major export of Thailand, the only country of the four with rice exports at all. It is dubious, given internal conditions and governmental dilemmas, that Thai rice exports can be significantly increased in the near future.

---

[37] FEER, (fn. 2), 26 March 1976, pp. 57-8.

[38] FEER Yearbook 1976, (fn. 9), p. 89.

[39] FEER, (fn. 2), 16 January 1976, p. 99.

Nevertheless they will certainly continue to be a major, probably the premier, commodity export. Malaysia, Indonesia, and the Philippines will probably not be Thailand's major rice importers past 1980. But there will be an ample market elsewhere in Asia. Maize, also an export exclusive to Thailand among these countries, has been increasing in export earnings dramatically, more than doubling from 1973 to 1974, and almost quadrupling since 1969. In 1974 it became the country's second highest export earner. Future prospects appear to be good.

ENVIRONMENTAL PERCEPTION AND RESOURCE BEHAVIOR IN THAILAND: A DEVELOPMENTAL DILEMMA

James A. Hafner

For over two decades the process of economic and social change in the developing world has been carefully subjected to microscopic analysis, monitoring, and at times even been guided by the more developed nations. Whether the motives and goals of this involvement can or have been justified is still a source of some doubt and continuing debate. There is little doubt, however, that many of the structural and technological requisites for economic and social change have been identified and documented. It has also been demonstrated that barriers to growth and causes of growth are often internal as well as external to a particular society.[1] Nevertheless, a dilemma persists in the continued slow progress of these nations towards achieving designated levels of growth after such a protracted period of technological and capital investment. One dimension of this dilemma which is immediately relevant to the future potential of natural resources in Southeast Asia continues to be elusive. This dimension concerns the role of perceptual views and attitudes which are held toward the environment and natural resources and the extent to which these views are manifest in patterns of resource use. The imprint of perceptual views on landscape and resources in East Asia is evident in the historical continuity of classical Chinese views of man-nature relations. In recent years Thailand has begun to confront a growing problem of resource abuse and mismanagement, yet there is almost a complete lack of information about how the environment and resources are perceived. The principal objective of this paper is to develop a framework for perceptual views of environment and resources in Thailand and to relate cognized views to the complex issues of resource use and development. Since the empirical basis for this discussion is from rural communities, a consideration of rural-urban differentials in perceptual views will not be attempted, nor is it suggested that elements of the perceptual framework can be extended to areas outside of Thailand. It is hoped, however, that this preliminary effort will both emphasize the importance of perception studies as a tool in understanding resource use behavior and suggest some areas for further study.

---

[1] Everett E. Hagen, _On the Theory of Social Change_ (Homewood, Ill.: The Dorsey Press, Inc., 1962).

The study of man's perception of space and environment has rapidly developed into a new and dynamic approach to the geographer's traditional concern for understanding man-environment relations. The foundation of this concept is based on the assumption that:

> environmental decisions and behavior are based on individual and group images of the real world. Thus, people presumably base their decisions not so much on the world as it is, but rather on the world as they perceive it.[2]

Man is seen in these terms as a decision maker and his behavior as some function of his subjective images of the real world formed from the composite inputs of his sensory and information processing mechanisms. Individually the effects of these decisions may be small, but when taken as an aggregate and as a cumulative process of entire populations of resource users their effects can be of considerable magnitude. The component elements of the perceptual mechanism suggests that factors causing individuals to see the same segment of reality differently may be seen as filters. Continual informational inputs are screened by these filters which would include language, social class, personal values, religious and belief systems, and some form of pattern-seeking function.[3] Behavior related to man's use of his environment and resources can therefore be better understood by investigating the bases upon which these perceptual views are founded.

The flexibility of this concept and its applications can be seen in the variety of topics and scales of inquiry found in the recent literature.[4] Immediately relevant here are several studies which treat landscape character and resource use patterns as functions of perceptual images and behavior. Tuan[5] has described in some detail the traditional Chinese attitudes towards nature and resources. As an

---

[2]T. F. Saarinen, "Environmental Perception," in Perspectives on Environment, eds., Ian R. Manners and Marvin W. Mikesell (Washington, D.C.: Association of American Geographers, 1974), p. 252.

[3]Downs has developed a conceptual schema of the perception mechanism which includes these filtering elements and allows for spatial and temporal variations in the perception process. See Roger M. Downs, "Geographic Space Perception: Past Approaches and Future Prospects," Progress in Geography 2 (1970): 65-108.

[4]Two recent reviews of perception research in geography and its applications can be found in L. J. Wood, "Perception Studies in Geography," Transactions of the Institute of British Geographers 5 (July 1970):129-42; and in Saarinen, "Environmental Perception," (fn. 2), pp. 252-89.

[5]Yi Fu Tuan, "Discrepancies Between Environmental Attitude and Behavior: Examples from Europe and China," Canadian Geographer 12 (1968): 176-91.

adaptive strategy towards the environment Chinese perceptual views have been embedded in philosophical, religious, and cosmological doctrines which emphasized man-nature harmonics. This complex of doctrine and related folklore provided one set of parameters for behavior toward resources. Patterns of resource exploitation which exceeded these boundaries jeopardized the essential balance in man-nature harmonics. That contradictions existed between stated ideals and behavior is strongly supported by Tuan's examples of deforestation in classical China. In an earlier paper Murphey[6] suggests that these contradictions may have been rationalized as being a cooperative maneuver designed to enrich nature by bringing more land under cultivation rather than being destructive. The persistence of contradictions between stated ideals and beliefs and patterns of resource use suggests one line of inquiry which may be relevant to the framework of perceptual views of resources in Thailand. A second area of focus suggested by these studies is the extent to which perceptual views and resource use behavior is linked to and embedded in religious and cosmological doctrine.

A somewhat different but related aspect of cognized views of man-nature relationships as reciprocal and reverential is found in the concept of Geopiety. Tuan has considered this concept as one which embodies, "the special complex of relations between man and nature involving emotional bonds typified by piety, propitiation, compassion, and affection," and where, "The recognition that duties and obligations are mutual extends beyond human relationships to nature."[7] Geopiety includes, then, relations not only among men, but also between man and the gods, or between man and nature, and is directed differentially to categories of nature depending on one's religious sophistication and position in society. It might be anticipated, therefore, that differences in perceptual views would covary within a spectrum of traditional to progressive religious orientation and with the status of the individual in the community and society.

The importance of tradition as one set of filters for man's perceptual images of landscape and resources has been emphasized by Hill's[8] study of landscape change

---

[6]Rhoads Murphey, "Man and Nature in China," Modern Asian Studies 1, No. 4 (1967): 313-33.

[7]Yi-Fu Tuan, "Geopiety: A Theme in Man's Attachment to Nature and to Place," in Geographies of the Mind, ed., J. Lowenthal and Martin Bowden (Oxford University Press, 1976), p. 14.

[8]David A. Hill, "The Process of Landscape Change: Bicultural Implications," in David A. Hill, The Changing Landscape of a Mexican Municipio: Villa Las Rosas, Chiapas, (Research Paper No. 91, Department of Geography, University of Chicago, 1964).

in southeastern Mexico. Tradition is seen as providing the basis for perception of a set of natural features as resources, and providing the fundamental technology and institutions for resource exploitation. Traditional beliefs, attitudes, and norms are one dimension of the Indian's more conservative view of landscape and his symbiotic relationship with the environment. Contrasts between the traditional subsistence resource use patterns of the Indian, and the parasitic commercial pursuits of the Ladino are seen by Hill to embody different sets of perceptual views. The persistence of milpa agriculture, even where alternative crops and wage labor are available, has been culturally consistent, and to paraphrase Redfield, was essential to participation in the moral and religious life of the community.[9] This practice, embedded in a reverence for nature and reinforced by strong traditions and supernatural beliefs in the power of nature, contributes to distinctly different sets of behavior toward the environment and natural resources.

In a more recent study of migration behavior in a rural Argentine community, Wilkie[10] has argued that perceptual views toward space and environment are elements of the villagers' orientation and are related to social class status within the community. Villagers of low social status have attitudes toward the environment characterized by high levels of mistrust, a dependence upon tradition rather than technology in dealing with environmental problems, personal behavior influenced by custom and group expectations, and low levels of spatial perception and mobility. Upper class villagers have a medium level of mistrust of their environment, exercise a wider use of technology, have poor spatial perception, and were peer directed in personal orientation. Villagers intermediate in status manifested a high trust in their environment, good spatial perception, and were more dependent upon their own resources in terms of dealing with resource problems and selection of migration destinations. The immediate implications of this typology are that social and economic status, as well as stage in life cycle of villagers, are correlated with perceptual views and behavior toward space, the environment, and natural resources. Through the process of mobility, traditional beliefs about the environment and resources are

---

[9]Robert Redfield, The Peasant Society and Culture (Chicago: University of Chicago Press, 1956): 64.

[10]Richard Wilkie, "Environmental Perception and Migration Behavior: A Case Study in Rural Argentina," (Paper presented at the Latin American Studies Association, Sixth Annual Meeting, Atlanta, Georgia, March 25-28, 1976.) To be published in Migration and Economic Development in the Third World, ed., Robert Thomas (East Lansing, Mich.: Michigan State University, Latin American Center, forthcoming).

progressively replaced by ones influenced more by scientific and technological factors. Although Wilkie emphasizes that the relationship between environmental and resource perception and status of the individual is not a linear one, the association between these factors is clearly defined. These diverse yet related themes, embedded in the influence of perceptual views on behavior, suggest several lines of inquiry appropriate to Thailand.

THE PERCEPTUAL FRAMEWORK

Studies of rural Thai attitudes and perceptual views of their environment and resources are almost totally lacking.[11] Some useful insights have been provided through the many ethnographic and community studies which emphasize the role of belief systems and social structure in patterning village behavior. However, much of this information is not presented with the objective of explaining resource behavior, although it can be useful in isolating some of the complex inputs which make up cognitive views of the environment. Recent data obtained during field work in Ayutthaya and Chonburi provinces in 1972-73 provide the basis for a more structured investigation of rural attitudes toward environment and resources. Several fundamental ideas about the villagers' attitudes toward their environment and resources were exposed during work in five villages in these provinces. These ideas are presented here as basic elements of the perceptual framework and are grouped into four categories: (1) traditional beliefs in environmental abundance and infinite resources, (2) man-nature harmonics, (3) resource use strategies, and (4) responsibility toward resource use and development. These factors are represented schematically in Figure 1 to emphasize the manner in which they reinforce one another and are embedded in various dimensions of the Thai cultural system. Consistent within each of these categories is evidence of contradictions between cognized views and behavior patterns, an aspect of the perceptual mechanism not unique to Thailand.

Traditional Beliefs in Environmental Abundance and Infinite Resources

The popular Thai saying, "rice on the land, fish in the waters," is widely quoted and understood to reflect a belief in the abundance of the environment. Stated in different terms it represents a belief in the infinite quality of natural resources without specific limits tied to levels of demand and exploitation.

---

[11] James A. Hafner, "Man and Environment in Rural Thailand," The Journal of the Siam Society 61, Part 2 (July 1973): 129-38.

Figure 1 - Schematic Structure of the Perceptual Mechanism in Thailand

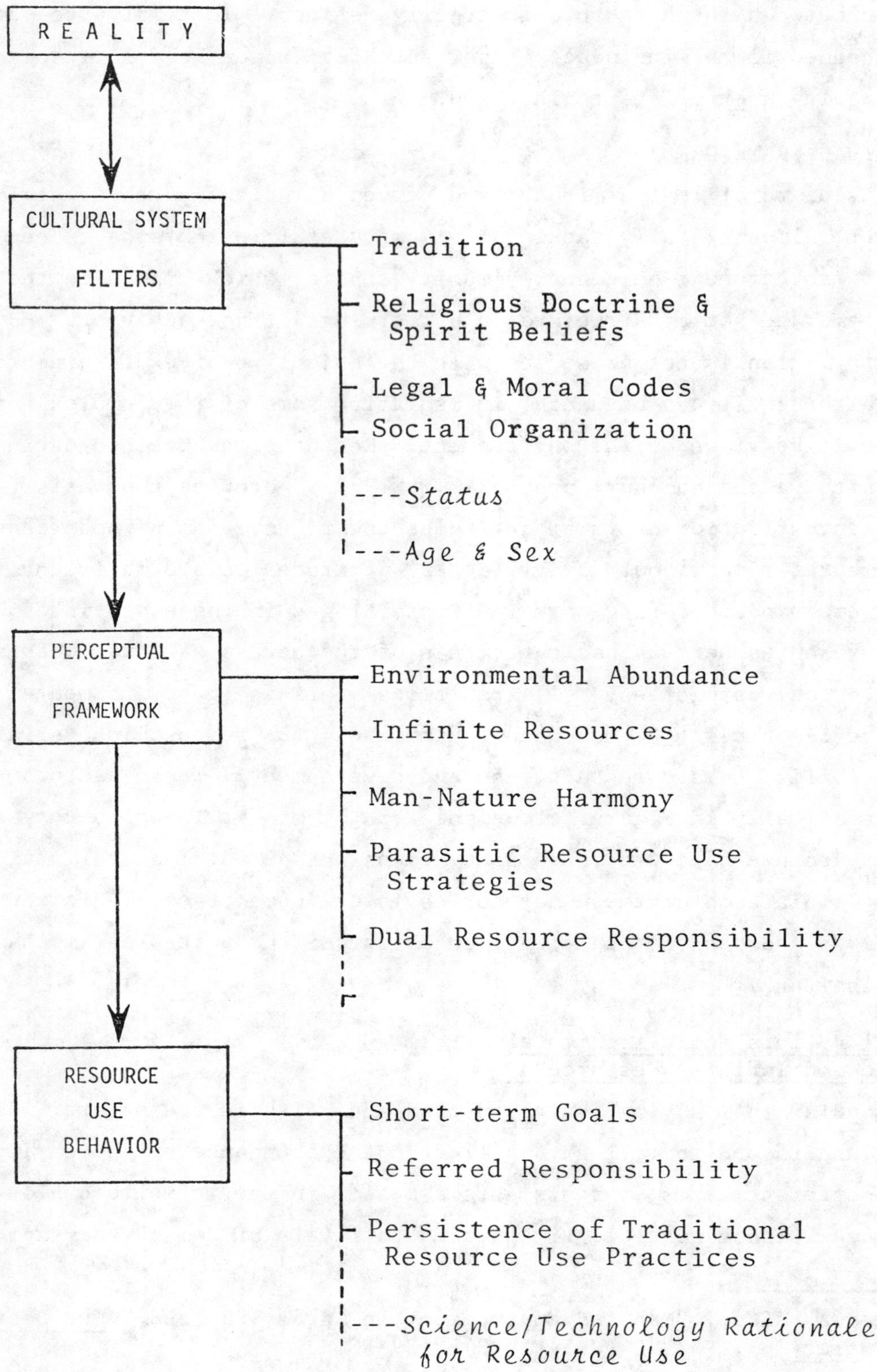

This traditional belief has deep historical roots dating to the 13th century and the reign of King Ramkhamhaeng.[12] That it has persisted as a popular expression of Thai beliefs and perceptions of their environment can be partly attributed to the absence of any evidence to contradict its basic truth. Its contemporary place in the perceptual framework of Thai villagers is evident in responses to queries about its degree of representation of current resource conditions. Over 60 per cent of the more than 124 household heads interviewed in five villages stated that this traditional belief was still an accurate representation of current conditions. Water, land, and forests were considered abundant, and although problems with each of these resources were apparent in the villages, only a minority perceived these problems. Among this minority, less than 20 per cent of those interviewed, most noted that fish populations had declined, insufficient water was available for irrigation, and soil fertility was poor. While this suggests that there may be a growing awareness of resource depletion, the majority view is one consistent with a belief in environmental abundance. These beliefs are also not confined to rural populations but can be found in statements of national leaders, and in some actions taken by government agencies. As recently as 1975, officials of the Forestry Department stated publicly that adequate reserved forest lands were available to accommodate new cooperative (nikhom) settlements, allow land under cultivation to be expanded, and settle evacuees from the proposed multi-purpose Pa Mong dam project.[13] However, subsequent studies have shown that squatting rates in national forest reserves and illegal logging since 1960 have reduced reserved forest land by over 30 per cent. Annual rates of decrease since 1970 from these two causes alone

---

[12]Coedes attributes this saying to an inscription contained on a monument erected during the reign of King Ramkhamhaeng in the late 13th century. G. Coedes, The Making of South East Asia (London: Routledge & Kegan Paul, 1966), p. 144. Wales also confirms that historically there is no evidence of food shortages or other indications of resource depletion which might have arisen to contradict this traditional belief in environmental abundance. See H. G. Quaritch Wales, Ancient Siamese Government and Administration (New York: Paragon Book Reprint Corporation, 1965).

[13]"Forest Reserve Land Available," Bangkok Post, March 20, 1975, p. 4. That this traditional belief is still widely held at many levels in Thai society is evident in a recent interview with Mr. Boonchu Rojanastien, a highly respected political and business leader. Bangkok Bank Monthly Review 16, No. 1 (January 1975): 25-26.

have been as high as 18 per cent in some regions of the country.[14] Similar statements concerning the availability of land for land reform have been made by officials of the land reform program in the Office of the Prime Minister. While these pronouncements may carry the weight of political expediency, they are embedded in a persistent belief in abundant and infinite natural resources. Thailand's chronic problems with over-cutting and illegal logging of its diminishing forest reserves, denuding of hillsides in the north and northeast, and problems with its agricultural water supply systems can be interpreted in terms of this persistent belief. A long historical continuity in the pervasive belief in environmental abundance can therefore be considered as one dimension of a Thai perceptual view of the environment.

Man-Nature Harmonics

Within the broad tradition of popular Thai folklore, spirit worship, and Buddhist cosmology is embedded an often explicit sense of man-nature unity and harmonics. The conception of the universe familiar to many literate Thais places man in a subordinate, yet not entirely dependent, position to nature.[15] Although the outward recognition of this relationship is not easily verbalized by the average villager, his behavior and participation in ritual observances which placate and appeal to the power of nature as a force are a recognition of this orientation. The frequently propitiated benevolent (_thewada_) and malevolent (_phii_) spirits, associated with planting and harvesting cycles, with rain making rituals, and with fields, pose the duality of this relationship. The _Bungbanfai_, or Rocket Firing Festival practiced in the northeast, represents one of the many examples of the symbolic unity of man and nature contained in myth and ritual. The myth associated with this annual festival tells of the origins of various swamps and rivers, all of which are of vital importance to the villagers who live in the dry northeastern region of the country. The central plot of the myth relates a contest between man and nature, represented symbolically in popular Buddhist folklore in the form of a water serpent (_Naga_). Nature, in the shape of a squirrel, is engaged

---

[14] Unpublished data, Department of Forestry, Government of Thailand and the United Nations Mekong Committee--Pa Mong Costing and Resettlement Project, University of Michigan (Ann Arbor).

[15] L. M. Hanks, "The Cosmic View of Bang Chan Villagers," _Proceedings, Ninth Pacific Science Congress_ 3, Anthropology and Social Sciences (Bangkok: 1957): 107-9.

in a rivalry with man for a female being, and on the ultimate death of the squirrel his flesh, which is inexhaustible, is consumed by the people. Tambiah[16] provides a detailed interpretation of the meaning of the myth and its symbolic and popular significance for the villager. He emphasizes that the underlying theme, ostensibly presented as a conflict between man and nature, actually states a complex relationship between the two. The overt antagonism between man and nature (Naga) reflects the futility of conflict where nature is eminently stronger than man. Nature, a power in its own right, is something with which man must learn to come to terms in order to insure prosperity, good health, and an orderly society. The opposition of man and nature is resolved through the consumption of the inexhaustible flesh of the squirrel [showing the symbolic dependence of man on nature, and reaffirming the ultimate abundance of the environment]. At one level of interpretation the myth shows a conflict between man and nature, with its superior force and destructive power. At a second level it establishes a relationship between man (or society) and nature; where both participate, and in which the union of man and nature is necessary to insure ordered society. Tambiah[17] sees myth and ritual as representing two coexisting ethical attitudes: of appeasement of a "father" [nature] by villagers who are his "children;" and of man, who is confronted by nature and must accept the fact of nature's power to harm as well as to reward. This symbolic representation of the man-nature relationship is widely found in many local, regional, and national ceremonies, and provides both a continuity and persistence in beliefs of environmental abundance and man's dependence on nature.[18] That contradictions of these perceptual views based on traditional beliefs are evident in Thai patterns of resource use is emphasized by the many recent examples of widespread abuse of natural resources.

Parasitic vs. Adaptive Resource Use Strategies

Considering the general absence of any widespread evidence to contradict

---

[16] S. J. Tambiah, *Buddhism and the Spirit Cults in North-east Thailand* (London: Cambridge University Press, 1970).

[17] *Ibid*., p. 309.

[18] Another ritual with an associated myth which is widely practiced throughout Thailand, The Story of the Female Spirit of Rice [*Nang Phrakosob*], links the domestication of rice to religion and associates religion with an ordered human existence. Rice and its cultivation are ethically and morally linked with Buddhism and behavior of the villager. *Ibid*., pp. 351-61.

traditional beliefs in environmental abundance, a related view is that man can and in fact does take at will from the environment. The general over-exploitation of natural resources without concern for their maintenance of conservation is unfortunately an increasingly common problem in Thailand and much of Southeast Asia.[19] Marine resources in the Gulf of Siam have reportedly declined by over 66 per cent since 1962 and industrial pollution of the Maekhlong and Tachin rivers caused over US$500,000 damage to marine life and soils in 1970 alone.[20] Similar problems can be identified in agricultural resource use patterns and the difficulties which have been encountered in diversifying the agricultural sector of the economy. These indications of parasitic rather than adaptive resource use strategies appear, at least initially, to be inconsistent with traditional beliefs and values. However, it can be argued that the basis for this contradiction and the frequent parasitic use of the environment is embedded in, and is consistent with, both the ethical structure and goal directed behavior found in Buddhist doctrine and the systems of spirit belief.

The imprint of Hinayance Buddhism on Thai life and culture is one of the most prominent characteristics of Thai society. Such fundamental concepts as merit (bun) and demerit (baab) play singularly important roles in the structuring of Thai behavior and perceptual views. Phillips places the role of this religious system in perspective by observing, ". . . Buddhism provides a corpus of knowledge for rationalizing and sanctioning certain types of behavior and for disapproving of others."[21] The intermingling of Buddhist doctrine, ethical concepts, and supernatural beliefs provides one basis for gaining insights into the manner in which the perceptual views and resource use behavior are both reinforced and sanctioned by these complex and pervasive belief systems.

Buddhism distinguishes between the worldly and the other worldly, illusion and reality, the material and the spiritual, suffering and the absence of

---

[19] A recent review and summary of environmental and resource problems in Thailand and Southeast Asia has been prepared by Gordon Conway and Jeff Romm, Ecology and Resource Development in Southeast Asia (Bangkok: The Ford Foundation, Office for Southeast Asia, 1973).

[20] Reported in an interview with the Director-General of the Fisheries Department. Bangkok Bank Monthly Review 13, No. 10 (October, 1972): 453.

[21] H. P. Phillips, Thai Peasant Personality (Berkeley: University of California Press, 1965), p. 90.

suffering. The fundamental message here is to renounce the world of reality and strive, through adherence to the precepts of Buddhism, to accumulate merit for an "other-worldly" spiritual reality and existence. The accumulation of merit is the basic path which must be followed to attain this goal. Traditional belief in spirits is exactly contrary to this, being concerned with worldly matters, such as avoidance of suffering, acceptance of the world as it is, and exploitation of the world's rewards.[22] If these two ethos are conflicting and incompatible, the persistence of spirit beliefs can be explained by the worldly-other worldly contradiction. Spirit beliefs provide a basis for behavioral actions which enable the villager to deal with reality and its material existence, including the use and manipulation of resources. There is no essential demerit in abusive resource use strategies or parasitic behavior toward the environment since these actions are a sanctioned means of accumulating the material wealth which enables the villager to make merit. Therefore, the economic (resource behavior) motivations of the villager, embedded in spirit beliefs, allow parasitic resource use strategies to exist as a means of accumulating merit. Numerous studies indicate that merit may be accumulated in different ways, however, the most widely sanctioned means require the expenditure of relatively large amounts of capital for _wat_ ordinations, _wat_ construction or repair, and _ngan tham bun_ or merit-making ceremonies.[23] For the villager it becomes an important ingredient of his behavioral motivation to accumulate wealth which will enable him to make the most meritorious types of

---

[22]A parallel and related argument for Burma has been posed by Spiro (1970). His arguments, greatly abbreviated here, are based on the proposition that frustration and aggression toward authority developed in childhood and reinforced by religious training enable the Burmese to cope with the resulting anxiety by transferring hostility to a belief in the supernatural (spirits). The natural world is then cognized as hostile, harmful, and populated by potentially malevolent and aggressive spirits which provides a motivational basis for behavior. Although he does not extend this motivational basis to behavior toward resources, it seems like a logical extension of the argument. See M. A. Spiro, _Buddhism and Society_ (New York: Harper and Row, Publishers, Inc., 1970).

[23]H. K. Kaufman, _Bangkhuad: A Community Study in Thailand_ (Locust Valley, N.Y.: J. J. Augustin, Incorporated, Publisher, 1960).

J. A. Niels Mulder, _Monks, Merit and Motivation_ (DeKalb, Ill.: Center for Southeast Asian Studies, Northern Illinois University, 1969).

Tambiah, _Buddhism_ . . . , (fn. 16).

Jane Bunnag, _Buddhist Monk, Buddhist Layman_ (London: Cambridge University Press, 1973).

contributions. That the villager does act toward the environment in a parasitic rather than symbiotic manner is consequently not inconsistent with these two systems, but is compatible with them. Symbiotic relationships in which man is an equal partner with nature rather than a parasite exist only infrequently, and the growing contradictions between traditional attitudes and behavior will continue to pose serious obstacles to any systematic efforts to promote better resource management through educational and conservation programs.

Responsibility Toward Resource Use and Development

A fourth general dimension of Thai perceptual views of environment and resources concerns their attitudes toward responsibility for resource conservation and development. These views appear to be polarized between the public vs. the private domain or to put it differently, between what is "mine" and what is "theirs." This distinction is probably not as clearly demarcated as in some Western nations, but is still evident in rural areas of Thailand. The assigning of responsibility for resource preservation and development is also qualified by moral and legal aspects of this responsibility. Villagers make clear choices between what resources fall into the public and private domain, and who is responsible for each. Over two-thirds of the sampled household heads assigned responsibility for natural resources to the government. This legal and official obligation was divided between the national government (43 per cent) and local village officials (24.2 per cent). However, villagers consistently included among public resources such elements as water, soils, rice fields, village paths and roads, and aquatic resources, many of which were clearly within the private domain. Only one-third of the villagers stated that private individuals, as resource users, were responsible for the resources they used, and a few even felt that no one was responsible for protecting and developing natural resources.

This apparent dichotomy between the villager's perceived role of government obligations toward resources and his own responsibilities can be tied to several factors. Moerman[24] and Keyes[25] have noted that a clear difference exists between

[24] M. Moerman, "The Village World and the Larger World," (Bangkok: United States Information Service, 1960). Mimeographed, 27 pp.

[25] C. Keyes, "Local Leadership in Thailand," in Local Authority and Administration in Thailand, eds., Fred R. von der Mehden and David A. Wilson (Los Angeles: Academic Advisory Council for Thailand, 1970), pp. 92-127.

the villager's view of government obligations and his own obligations. Distinctions are made between obligations to participate in community-wide resource conservation and development projects, and the responsibility of the government to carry out these programs. This contrast in responsibility seems particularly evident where political participation and involvement is limited.[26] However, Keyes[27] notes that throughout Thailand, and even in the central plain, political participation and involvement in community action programs is effectively nonexistent. Divergent views of personal (moral) obligations and governmental (legal) responsibilities contribute to a persistent lack of involvement in fundamental resource preservation and development activities among rural villagers. Reciprocity, a basic construct within Thai social structure, is an important factor in these attitudes. In attempting to keep the government at a distance and to avoid its services and obligations the villager, through reciprocal constructs, thinks in terms of short-term, self-interest relations. Local resource conservation practices which are not consistent with this short-term, self-interest view are simply not part of the villager's perceptual and behavioral framework toward natural resources.

The moral dimension of this dilemma of responsibility can be emphasized by the concept of duty (nathi). The villager's duty is essentially determined by social and economic conditions beginning at birth which contribute to a definition of his personal sphere of responsibility.[28] This fundamental moral duty, reinforced by Buddhist teachings, places great emphasis on responsibility to one's family and neighbors, but excludes any extension of this obligation to the government. The villager may, therefore, feel no obligation to assume a duty, accept a responsibility, or contribute to a project which he perceives of as not appropriately his own. Duty as perceived by the villager may then be manifest in terms of his lack of responsibility toward the care and conservation of public resources, the principal obligation for which is embedded in legal codes and traditions which assign this responsibility to local officials and the national government. And,

---

[26] A more detailed study of the conflicts in authority and responsibility between villager and government can be found in von der Mehden and Wilson, eds., Local Authority . . . (fn. 25).

[27] Keyes, "Local Leadership . . ." (fn. 25), pp. 123-6.

[28] Stephen B. Young, "Northeastern Thai Village: Non-Participatory Democracy," Asian Survey 8, No. 11 (1968): 873-86.

unlike classical China where Taoist and Confucian philosophies clearly elaborated the importance of man's moral and ethical responsibilities toward his environment, popular Buddhism seems to take no explicit position on this issue. Few villagers were able to identify any moral or ethical guidelines, stemming from their knowledge of Buddhist teachings, which related to behavior toward resources. There are of course strong prohibitions against taking life in any form, yet there are no apparent moral sanctions related to man's behavior toward other elements of the natural environment. Where villagers perceive of their responsibilities toward natural resources in these terms, which impose little or no obligation on themselves, over-exploitative and non-adaptive behavior in resource use can be the ultimate result. This apparent absence of moral and legal responsibility toward the environment and a heavy loading of obligations toward the legal and "official" position of the government appears to be a central component of Thai perceptual views of their environment.

The perceptual framework as proposed here and outlined tentatively in Figure 1 consists of several basic elements. The fundamental components of this view include a traditional belief in environmental abundance and infinite natural resources, in the harmony of man with nature embedded in philosophical and cosmological views which insures an orderly worldly life but imposes no sanctions on parasitic resource use behavior, in the absence of symbiotic relationships in natural resource use practices, and in a dual framework of responsibility toward resource preservation and development, weighted heavily toward the moral and legal obligations of the government.

ENVIRONMENTAL ORIENTATION AND BEHAVIOR: A TENTATIVE MODEL

The rural Thai perceptual view of environment and resources as proposed here should not be considered to be uniformly manifest in every community or among all individuals in every village. Varying social, economic, philosophical, and spatial orientations among individuals suggests that perceptual views and resource use behavior are more dynamic than static. Changes in individual perceptual views may occur with shifts in social status, in economic position, or in degree of spatial mobility, or because of a general modification of the system of cultural filters through which the environment is perceived. Perceptual views can then be expected to vary among individuals within a community or society based on their social and economic status, age, and sex.[29] This dimension of the perceptual equation in Thailand provides a framework for a preliminary model of Environmental Orientation and Behavior. It must be emphasized, however, that the proposed model should be considered only as a suggestive rather than definitive conceptualization which will enable diverse yet related sets of factors to be organized in a more systematic manner (Figure 2).

A continuum of perceptual views from Traditional to Progressive is proposed as one dimension of the model, based on analysis of village attitude samples. These contrasting poles represent two diverse but linked extremes in perceptual views and environmental orientation. The Traditional orientation is consistent with beliefs in environmental abundance and infinite resources, high levels of mistrust of the natural environment, a dependence upon natural forces and traditional practices to maintain man-nature harmony, resource use behavior directed by traditional values and beliefs which allows for parasitic resource use strategies, and the assigning of responsibility for resources to the legal and official role of the government and its agencies. The opposing Progressive orientation embodies an awareness of finite resources, technological and scientific solutions to environmental and resource problems, responsibility for resources as a shared obligation of the individual and government, and an outward rejection of traditional values and beliefs related to the man-nature relationship. These two extremes in orientation are represented in Figure 2 on the horizontal scale. The intermediate position between these two poles is the area of greatest dynamics in environmental orientation and behavior. The vertical dimension of Figure 2 represents a general indicator of individual status within the community. This indicator was defined by a range of economic, social, and spatial variables.[30] Villagers of low status within the community are generally equated with a more traditional orientation toward the environment while those of intermediate and high status exhibit attitudes and behavior which is more progressive, dynamic, and flexible, relative to the traditional pole.

Attitudinal samples among rural villagers tend to confirm the broad outlines

---

[29] Wilkie, "Environmental Perception . . . ," (fn. 10).

[30] Status within the community was operationally determined from (a) formal and informal positions held within the community, (b) size of operational farm holdings, (c) disposable income from agriculture, (d) amount and sources of non-farm, off-farm income, and (e) demographic characteristics of the household.

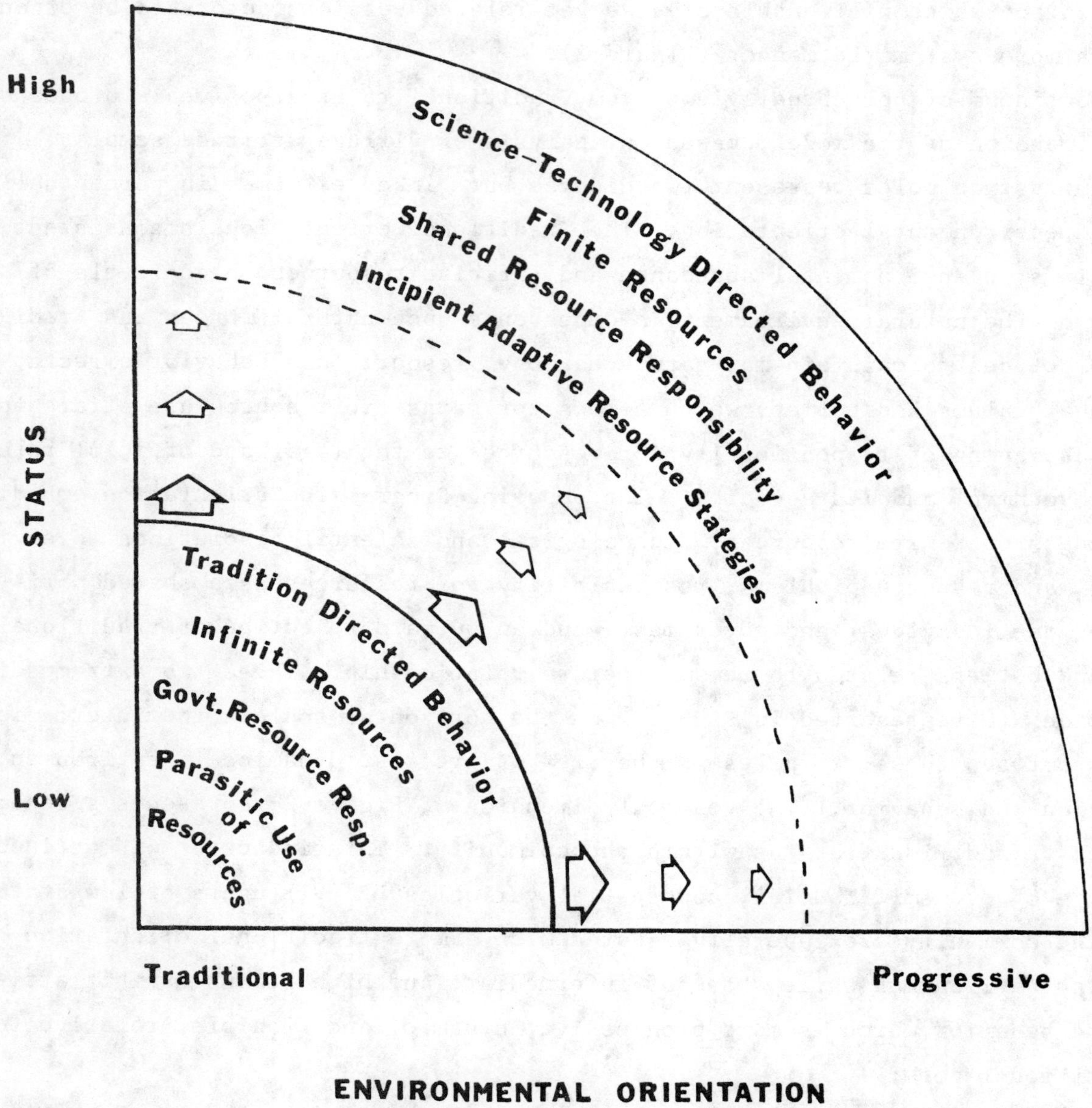

Fig. 2 - A MODEL OF ENVIRONMENTAL ORIENTATION AND BEHAVIOR

of the proposed model. Villagers of low status were strongly tradition directed in attitudes and behavior toward their environment and natural resources. The majority of these villagers were small-scale, wet-rice farmers who depended exclusively on traditional cropping patterns and techniques and received no income from off-farm, non-farm employment. They consistently agreed that resources were abundant and infinite, and few associated growing problems of resource shortages within the village to past and current resource use practices. They deplored the high cost of charcoal and lumber and remarked on the absence of trees within the village, yet did not associate these problems with past practices of forest clearance and the use of vegetative resources. Solutions to these problems were consequently seen to be embedded in traditional practices of spirit worship, propitiation, and ritual observances. They also agreed that moral and legal responsibility for resources lay with local officials, government agencies, and the national government. Evidence of a fundamentally parasitic view of resource use was contained in their rejection of various forms of innovative technology (fertilizers, insecticides), the belief that "fields and rice are for us to use," and the often stated feeling that "when we are hungry we must do something." This complex of perceptual views was also supported by low spatial perception and very limited spatial mobility. The frequency of non-farm employment and travel outside of the village was the lowest among these individuals. The villager of low status, however, appeared to have a significantly higher local environmental awareness than individuals of intermediate or high status.[31]

Many of the more affluent, high status villagers possess views and attitudes which are characterized by some Thai scholars in terms of the notion of "western scientific man."[32] Beliefs in environmental abundance and infinite resources are

---

[31]Delane Welsch has commented that Thai rice farmers have a general lack of knowledge about their environmental resource base. While this observation conflicts with empirical data on local environmental and spatial familiarity among villagers in Ayutthaya, it is not inconsistent with the generally observed absence of symbiotic resource use strategies. See Delane Welsch, "Some Speculations on the Long Run Future of Rice in Thailand," Bangkok Bank Monthly Review 13, No. 3 (March 1972): 102-03.

[32]Pataya Saihoo, "Beliefs, Values and Goals of Farmers in Relation to Agricultural Development," Journal of Social Science 11, No. 1 (January 1974): 39-53.

Sasidhorn Nibondh, "Major Social Problems and Group Dynamics in Thai Society," (Chiengmai: unpublished manuscript, 1973).

generally rejected and traditional attitudes toward the power of nature over man are often labelled as "old fashioned" and "not scientific" by this group of villagers. These individuals were consistently large land owners who cultivated wet-rice, corn, and cash crops, occupied positions of high status in the village, and invested surplus capital and labor in diverse agricultural and non-farm activities. This group of villagers also showed a general awareness of problems of resource depletion, and interposed science and technology between man and nature as the appropriate solutions to these problems. Traditional remedies based on beliefs in the supernatural were seldom expressed, although it is unlikely that they have been discarded entirely. Pataya Saihoo[33] has argued that traditional beliefs and values are one of the major barriers to the development of new patterns of resource use but cannot be seen as entirely responsible for the absence of development among rural farmers. Bunnag[34] asserts in her study of popular Buddhism in Ayutthaya that the more progressive lay Buddhist scorns orthodox religious elements and views science as a more effective means of dealing with many problems. A similar position has been taken by Spiro[35] who states that urban Burmese are skeptical of spirits and traditional beliefs in the supernatural, but will express at least tacit recognition of these traditional life forces.

The dual responsibility toward environment and resources, which is a component of Thai perceptual views, is evident among higher status villagers. Responsibility is framed in terms of a shared obligation on the part of both the government and the individual. Legal obligations are still heavily weighted toward the government, but these villagers more frequently saw this obligation as one which included the private individual as well. Moral directives within Buddhism to respect one's neighbors' possessions were often interpreted to include both his household belongings and his property, as well as those resources which fell into the public domain. The extension of this moral obligation beyond personal property and resources may be partly attributed to somewhat more liberal interpretations of these teachings by some local Buddhist monks. The movement toward a more "scientific" view of resource use and maintenance among the higher status villagers

---

[33] Saihoo, "Beliefs, Values . . . ," (fn. 32), p. 64.

[34] Bunnag, Buddhist Monk . . . , (fn. 23), p. 148.

[35] Spiro, Buddhism and Society, (fn. 22), p. 62.

appears to have fostered the fundamental notion that finite resources require a more adaptive and symbiotic strategy in their use. However, within the view of these individuals although resources were considered as finite it was assumed that technology and science could be employed to sustain them. Consequently, parasitic behavior in resource use was not precluded, but was observed in patterns of irrigation water use in several villages.

This rather skeletal model of Environmental Orientation and Behavior is an attempt to juxtapose basic elements of a Thai perceptual view of environment and resources with certain fundamental dynamics of the rural community. At this preliminary stage little can be said regarding the dynamics and modification of traditional views among intermediate status villagers. A refinement of this aspect of the model is expected to be possible as data analysis proceeds. There is sufficient evidence at this point, however, to suggest that perceptual views as a dynamic element in village resource behavior are both contributory and inhibiting dimensions of the patterns of resource use in rural Thailand. It remains now to consider some of the implications of these perceptual views and their related behavior for the future of resource use.

PERCEPTION AND RESOURCE DEVELOPMENT: A CONTINUING DILEMMA

The fundamental dilemma posed by this outline of perceptual views of environment and natural resources is in many ways not new nor entirely unique to Thailand. This dilemma has been confronted, in one form or another, by planners, government officials, and national leaders in Thailand for many years. The basis of this dilemma is the persistence of traditional and potentially counter-productive resource use strategies, which have impaired progress toward nationally defined resource use goals and priorities. There exists an extensive list of documented reasons for this persistent dilemma, many of which impinge directly or indirectly on the effects of perceptual views on this problem. It is our contention at this point that as long as the full dimensions of the perceptual mechanism in Thailand are inadequately understood this dilemma will continue to pose barriers to planned economic change. A review of a few of the implications of perceptual views of resources, as they have been stated here, may help to both clarify and emphasize the importance of this problem.

Agricultural diversification is one of the basic priorities which has been established for the Thai economy. This involves an increased emphasis on non-traditional crops and a shift of resources to the production of commodities with stronger markets such as fibres, industrial oils, and export based crops. Diversification has proceeded slowly and has been plagued by a lack of resource mobility, unrealistic market price structures, a lack of suitable alternative crops, and the persistence of traditional resource use practices. For the many farmers which are tradition directed in their attitudes towards and use of resources, programs aimed at diversification of resource use conflict with these views. Development of new cropping systems presents a contradiction of traditional practices sanctioned by beliefs, values, religious philosophies, and perceptual views. Although some evidence is available to confirm that farmers are responsive to new cropping systems where market and price incentives are present, only modest changes from rice to other crops have been recorded in the past fifteen years. In some instances resources taken out of irrigated and upland rice have reverted back to this traditional cropping system. Resolution of this basic dilemma must involve a more intensive and comprehensive educational program which will address both the technical and attitudinal dimensions of agricultural diversification.

The persistent lack of participation in the developmental goals and programs of the country by the rural population in general is another aspect of this dilemma. The general inability of development programs to encourage more popular participation also has some foundation in the cognized views of responsibility and obligation for resource use and development. Only recently has there been any evidence of a willingness to shift some of the responsibility and decision making for resource use and planning to groups directly concerned with these issues. The recently implemented "Tambon Scheme" of the former Kukrit administration is the most notable example.[36] Although it is too early to adequately evaluate this program, or even to question how the recent change in government will affect its implementation, programs of this type may well help to change cognized views of

---

[36] The "Tambon Scheme" was formalized on April 1, 1975 and involves providing Baht 2,500 million (US$125 million) to rural tambon councils to fund various resource and community development projects conceived and carried out by the rural community. Some initial evaluations and critiques of the program can be found in The Investor 7, No. 6 (June 1975): 21-34; and Jonathan Swift, "Tambon Council Projects, An Overwhelming Success," Bangkok Post, July 6, 1975, Sec. II, p. 11.

the environment and responsibility for resource use and development.[37] Where the investment of capital resources and planning authority is placed more directly in the hands of local officials and villagers it may be expected that traditional self-interest of the villager and the referred responsibility toward resource conservation may become less significant barriers to resource development and conservation.

The continued belief among rural Thais in a cosmological order where man is dominated by nature and where these beliefs are reinforced by popular folklore, spirit beliefs, and Buddhist doctrine has also served to slow programs urging more effective and non-traditional uses of resources. A modification of these views to enable villagers to see the alternatives for resource use in a more adaptive and symbiotic way is not an easily resolved problem. The experience of the People's Republic of China in reversing the polarity of the traditional man-nature equation has produced impressive results. Thought reform and re-education have developed entirely new sets of attitudes and perceptual views which have been manifest in agricultural and industrial development programs.[38] The Democratic People's Republic of Kampuchea (Cambodia) by all recent reports is embarked on a similar course. Daily broadcasts of Phnom Penh radio exhort the citizens "to defend and build a new Kampuchea," and to become "masters of nature, masters of the country, and masters of the rice paddies and the fields." Peasants are urged to ". . . take their destiny in hand, in all circumstances and areas without counting on heaven or nature any more."[39] The outcome of this massive social and political experiment is uncertain, but the necessity to overcome and restructure traditional perceptual views of resources is clearly evident. Such a radical program is not proposed for

---

[37]The Yung Yai poaching scandal of 1973 has awakened interest in the need to preserve national forest reserves and the valuable wildlife found in these areas. The Director of the Division of Wildlife Management, Royal Forest Department, has recently taken a new and unique step toward solving this problem, the establishment of a Nature Education Centre at the Khao Chong Forest Reserve in Phatthalung and Satun provinces in the south. This initial effort is a first step toward implementing an improved wildlife law since as long as the population does not understand and appreciate the importance of these natural resources they will not abide by laws designed to protect and encourage more effective development of these resources.

[38]Murphey, "Man and Nature . . . ," (fn. 6).

[39]François Ponchaud, "Cambodia Under the Lash," Atlas World Press Review 23, No. 5 (May 1976): 16-19.

Thailand. However, there is a basic truth here concerning the relationship between cognized views of the world and its resources and the relative success of efforts to generate more efficient resource use patterns. Thailand could well benefit from the lesson, and in doing so anticipate less conflict with traditional attitudes as barriers to the growing need for a more adaptable pattern of resource conservation and development.

THE PLANTATION AS THE MODEL FOR PIONEER SETTLEMENT SPONSORED BY THE MALAYSIAN GOVERNMENT

Karl J. Pelzer

Agricultural pioneering throughout the world has the reputation of being a back-breaking undertaking characterized by hunger, malnutrition, poor housing, and deprivation of various kinds, such as safe drinking water, adequate schooling, roads, clinics, and hospitals. And still the pioneer is driven by his ambition to better the future of his children, even at the risk of his own life. He spends years clearing the forest, taming the land, and getting it ready for the cultivation of wet-rice, should he be a pioneer in the Asiatic tropics.

In a very concise way a German saying describes the fate of a pioneering family. "Der Erste hat den Tod, der Zweite hat die Not, der Dritte hat das Brot." (The First reaps death, the Second deprivation, the Third bread.) For it is not until the third generation takes over, benefiting from the toil of the preceding generations, that the family becomes established and has an adequate income.

Before World War II spread to the Pacific, I had the opportunity to study government-sponsored agricultural pioneer settlement in the Philippines and in the Netherlands East Indies. The contrast between the aid that the Philippines' and the Netherlands East Indies' governments rendered to their respective settlers is quite striking and is briefly commented upon in the following pages.

In 1968, I studied the settlement schemes of the Malaysian Federal Land Settlement Authority in Western Malaysia. It is my intention to compare prewar government-sponsored pioneering projects in the Philippines and the Netherlands East Indies with the postwar settlement schemes in Malaysia.

Pioneering in the Philippines

Just before World War II the Commonwealth Government aimed at opening Mindanao as rapidly as possible, while at the same time avoiding past mistakes in the field of agricultural colonization. "The Commonwealth Government . . . decided to concentrate first on a program of extended road-building and public-land surveying before again attempting to establish government-supported agricultural colonies."[1]

[1] K. J. Pelzer, Pioneer Settlement in the Asiatic Tropics. Studies in Land Utilization in Southeastern Asia, (New York, New York: 1945), p. 135.

Manuel Roxas, Chairman of the National Economic Council, reporting to President Quezon on October 22, 1938, criticized earlier attempts:

> In no instance had there proceeded a careful study and selection of land to be settled nor of the people that were to be given State help to settle on those lands. No thought was apparently given to the important question of marketing of products of new settlers, neither was there any well-thought-out plan of assisting them to become efficient producers by providing for them demonstration and experimental stations or equipping them with modern tools and implements.[2]

Roxas proposed the organization of the National Land Resettlement Corporation, later renamed National Land Settlement Administration (NLSA). Its objectives were formulated as follows: (1) Settlement of young reservists in unpeopled regions in order to strengthen the defense of the thinly settled parts of the islands; (2) Movement of tenant farmers in order to improve conditions in those provinces where agrarian disputes and unrest were most frequent; (3) Filipinization of non-Christian Filipinos and their amalgamation with Christian Filipinos; (4) Development of new export crops in order to insure the country against economic reverses that might otherwise result from independence.[3]

Commonwealth Act No. 441, of June 3, 1939, following the lines that Roxas had proposed, incorporated the main objectives in the following terms:

(a) To facilitate the acquisition, settlement, and cultivation of lands whether acquired from the Government or from private parties;

(b) To afford opportunity to own farms to tenant farmers and small farmers from congested areas, and to trainees who have completed the prescribed military training;

(c) To encourage immigration to sparsely populated regions, and facilitate the amalgamation of the people in different sections of the Philippines;

(d) To develop new money crops to take the place of the present export crops, which may suffer from the loss of preferences which they enjoy in the American market.[4]

NLSA was obliged to advance the cost of sea transportation to Dadjangas, in Mindanao; to assign to the settler 12 hectares (30 acres) of agricultural land; to

---

[2] *Ibid.*, p. 137.

[3] *Ibid.*, p. 137, footnote 17.

[4] Philippines (Commonwealth), Commonwealth Act No. 441, June 3, 1939, Sec. 2.

provide him, on a credit basis, with building material for his house, food until he was self-supporting, and the use of machinery such as tractors and plows, which would make it easy to break the sod of the Koronadal Valley.

The contract favored the settler, relieving him of most of the usual hazards and burdens of pioneering. NLSA avoided heavily forested areas, choosing instead cogonales, or grass-covered areas. The availability of modern agricultural machinery took the sting out of pioneering. Tractor-powered plows broke the sod and readied the land in record time for cultivation. Although the first settlers received 12 hectares (about 30 acres), by 1940 the land allotment was cut in half--since Filipino farmers are hardly capable of cultivating 30 acres. The management of NLSA envisaged that the settlers use half of the land for the cultivation of subsistence crops such as upland or lowland rice, maize, sweet potatoes, and cassava, and the other half for cash crops such as coffee, cacao, cotton, soy beans, peanuts, cowpeas, Bermuda onions, and other crops for which there was a market in the Philippines.

Pioneering in the Netherlands East Indies

By comparison with the pioneer settlers of the Philippines, those of the Netherlands East Indies were given only a bare minimum of support. In the period between 1932 and 1941 the settler received nothing free except his land, and that amounted to only a small home lot and two acres of potential wet-rice land. The clearing of either primeval or secondary growth forest land fell upon the settlers, who needed at least two years to complete the task. Transportation from Java to the Outer Islands, as well as household utensils and tools such as axes and bush knives and agricultural implements were advanced but had to be paid back within a two- or three-year period. Although a Javanese settler in his fourth year in Sumatra was considerably better off than he had been in Java, provided his land had been brought under irrigation, he had not prospered as much as the Filipino pioneer settler in Mindanao who received much more land and could rent agricultural machinery from the machine pool of NLSA.

Pioneer Settlement in Malaysia

During the postwar period the Government of Malaysia became very much aware that tens of thousands of Malays and smaller numbers of Malaysian citizens of Chinese and Indian extraction were either landless or so land-poor that they could hardly support themselves. In 1956, during the First Five-Year Plan, which covered the years 1956-1960, the Malayan Government established the Federal Land Development Authority (FLDA, subsequently known as FELDA) with the mandate to redeem the newly elected government's promise to resettle landless citizens.

As one would expect, during the nearly twenty years of its operations FELDA made numerous changes in order to improve its efficiency. In the early days FELDA expected the settlers to clear the forest themselves, plant their own export crops, build their own houses, and develop their own kitchen gardens. This placed a very heavy burden on the settlers and forced them to be true pioneers. No wonder that progress in the pioneering communities was disappointingly slow. Up until 1961 FELDA operated only as a planning and financing agency. It examined the suitability of each settlement project offered by a state government, planned its development, decided which cash crops were to be planted, and provided the necessary funds on a loan basis. At this point FELDA's responsibilities ceased, the administration of each project being then transferred to a state development board responsible to the state in which the scheme was located. This meant that there was no unity in the administration; and some of the states were unable to run the schemes effectively.

FELDA, however, was dissatisfied with the selection and performance of the settlers. District officers tended to rid themselves of troublesome persons in their areas by shipping them off to the settlement projects. No wonder that the quality of the settlers did not speak well for the expected advancement of the settlement schemes.

But in 1961 a very important change took place. The National Land Council made FELDA directly responsible for the inception and administration of all schemes under the Land Development Ordinance. FELDA, with the consent of the state concerned, took over the management of all thirteen FELDA-financed state schemes, of which four were located in Kedah, one in Trengganu, three in Malacca, and five in Johore. A fourteenth scheme, located in Kelantan, was not taken over on account of a conflict between that state and the federal government.

The Malayan planners were never interested in subsistence agriculture of the type developed in the Indonesian and Philippine settlement projects either before or after World War II. Instead they stressed commercial, export-oriented agriculture with palm oil, palm kernel, rubber, and, most recently, sugar cane as main crops.

In 1961 two federal committees, the Technical Investigation Committee and the Technical Planning Committee, were established to assist in the preliminary investigation of proposed schemes and in the planning of selected schemes, respectively. The main function of the Investigation and Planning Committees is to coordinate all services required in FELDA projects at the federal level. The Technical Investigation

Committee assesses the suitability of land offered by one of nine states, so far as topography and soils are concerned. In particular it must determine whether the soil is best suited for rubber or for oil palm. In very large projects involving tens of thousands of acres, the soil scientists have to distinguish between areas best suited for rubber and for oil palm, since the value of palm oil and palm kernel produced per acre is higher than the value of rubber produced per acre. When one adds that oil palms reach the production stage in four years, while rubber trees reach the tapping age in seven, it is obvious that oil palms should be given preference over rubber provided the soil quality is right. Mineral, agricultural, and forest clearance must be obtained. To illustrate the last point: should the Bureau of Mining have evidence that the area under consideration contains extensive alluvial bodies of tin ore, the land would not be released for settlement under FELDA auspices because of the tin deposits.

FELDA prefers, for economic reasons, to use the services of existing government agencies whenever possible. Soil surveys are undertaken by the Department of Agriculture, land survey and aerial photography by the Survey Department, drainage by the Drainage and Irrigation Department, village designs by the Town and Country Planning Department, roads and water supplies by the Public Works Department, schools by the Ministry of Education, clinics by the Ministry of Health, and passenger transport by the Council of Trust for Indigenous People (MARA).

Again in 1961-62, a very important decision was made to speed up the development of settlement schemes. Instead of having the settlers carry out the pioneer work of felling the forest, planting either rubber or oil palms, and building their houses on land set aside for the villages, FELDA decided to use Chinese contractors, who submitted their financial bids for clearing the jungle, planting rubber trees, oil palms and cover crops, building roads through the agricultural areas and villages, and for constructing houses for staff members and villagers. The contractors were also responsible for the maintenance of the trees and cover crops for half a year to a year until the arrival of the settlers in the villages of the respective projects. Since the Chinese employ fellow countrymen, the Chinese community is thus compensated for the virtual absence of Chinese in the FELDA settlement schemes. (Only in the Bilut scheme in western Pahang do we find both Chinese and Indians side by side with Malay settlers. Even here the Malays are in a majority.)

Terracing, where slope conditions call for it, and tree planting under the supervision of the contractor and his staff and inspected by FELDA experts assure a uniformity which can be achieved by plantations but not by pioneer small holders. Most impressive is the use of labor-saving machinery: power saws, trucks for the hauling of valuable trees to saw mills, bulldozers for clearing the land and the construction of terraces. Since FELDA selects only large blocks of over 3,000 and usually up to 4,000 or 5,000 acres, (more recently the giant Jengka Triangle block of about 100,000 acres was selected), FELDA can hardly be distinguished from plantations owned by corporations. The planting instructions have been modeled after those of plantations and a high percentage of the managerial personnel was previously employed by plantations.

All the truly taxing pioneering work is performed by the labor-groups of Chinese contractors. The Malay settlers arrive about 2 to 2½ years after the initiation of the projects in the settlements, where they find houses in one of two designs, and commercial and cover crops already planted and maintained until their arrival. Thus, the struggle has been taken out of pioneering. As a matter of fact the settlers come into ready-made beds; all of the work which a pioneer faces when he enters a pioneer settlement is already done. Instead he acknowledges his account with FELDA which includes the cost of clearing, of planting the commercial crops and the cover crops, and of the house.

FELDA concentrates on the training of efficient rubber tappers and oil palm cultivators, although it pays lip service to the need for a diversification of agriculture. In reality, it pays almost no attention to the broader problems of training the settlers in general agricultural techniques in order to develop all-round skilled farmers. Although as much as 15-20 per cent of the land in a scheme is set aside for fruit gardens (<u>dusuns</u>) and other crops, FELDA concentrates on the cash crops. In 1963, only 5 per cent of the land designated for small crops had actually been planted. As a matter of fact, FELDA lacked instructors who would have been able to help the settlers with the development of secondary crops. Since rubber, in the early days the most important crop, came under the Department of Commerce rather than the Department of Agriculture, the latter was only marginally involved in the agricultural development of FELDA projects. FELDA left the assignment of training the settlers to become efficient farmers, capable of looking after commercial as well as subsistence food crops, to the extension services of the Agriculture and Veterinary Departments. The clearing contracts did not include the so-called <u>dusun</u> land which was to supply the settlers with fruit, vegetables, and other small crops. FELDA expected the settlers to clear the <u>dusun</u> and plant such fruit trees as mango, mangistan, durian, citrus trees, avocado, and other fruit trees. However, in most settlement schemes the dusun areas were only partially cleared and very poorly maintained. In some projects extensive amounts of land suitable for wet-rice cultivation had been cleared and were regularly used. The first love of the Malay farmers belongs to wet-rice.

In the course of an interview, a high official of the Department of Agriculture recalled that FELDA for economic and political reasons favored rubber in the early years, oil palm for the same reasons in recent years. In the late sixties and early seventies, one-third of the land was planted with rubber and two-thirds with oil palm. Good rice land was converted into rubber gardens despite the expense of draining the land. This official charged that very steep land was planted with rubber without proper terracing--clean weeding was practiced--and Malays who did not follow the example of the European planter were ridiculed and accused of being lazy.

This spokesman for the Department of Agriculture raised the question:

> Should we not think of genuine diversification of agriculture? We should stimulate the production of corn, tapioca, coffee, cacao, soybean, peanuts, fruit trees such as the various citrus trees, avocado, and mango, to mention only a few. We should reduce imports from Thailand and Australia in order to protect the domestic producer wherever possible. The Department of Agriculture was never given adequate encouragement, funds, and personnel to foster small-holder agriculture or to carry on research in food crops--rubber was King and everybody had to pay his respects to His Majesty. And now the country goes mad over oil palm; the Department of Agriculture is accused of having neglected its duties and is not in a position to meet the demand for seed material.

This interview provides ample evidence of the jealousy and rivalry between the Department of Agriculture and FELDA. In the competition, the Department of Agriculture is out-matched budget-wise. All that it can do is to point to shortcomings in management, such as the neglect of the production of staple and secondary crops. In many instances settlers are not yet self-supporting several years after entering their new villages because the dusun land is not yet in production.

In order to provide the necessary livelihood, FELDA pays the head of the household M$2.90 a day. Should the wife help she receives M$2.40; children between 14 and 18 years of age receive M$1.50 and children under 14, M$1.00. A man working the expected 24 days a month thus draws M$69.60. This amount increases if other members of his family share in the work.

On entering the settlement project each settler is nominally provided with 10 acres (it used to vary from 6 to 8 acres) of rubber or oil palm and a house on a

¼-acre lot. The settler, however, does not know the exact location of his 10 acres. Settlers begin to maintain cash crops on a collective basis with 15 - 20 settlers assigned to a particular block of land. They carry out such works as weeding, fertilizing, pest and disease control, and pruning under the supervision of FELDA management staff, who have been resident in the project since the very beginning. When rubber is about five or six years old the individual lots are surveyed and subsequently allocated to individual settlers and are entered into the Register of Holdings. By now the 10-acre rubber lots no longer require 24 days of maintenance but only 12 - 14 days at the most. FELDA expects that settlers work in the dusun area, participate in the construction of fish ponds, or in the development of wet-rice fields in order to qualify for M$69.60 per month maintenance allowance.

Once the settler can begin to tap his rubber trees, the payment of maintenance allowance stops. Instead he now begins to make loan repayments for the support he has received from FELDA.

Loans received by the Settler from FELDA

1) Cost of clearing the land and the planting of the main crops inclusive of maintenance by a contractor until settler arrival;
2) Cost of fertilizers, chemicals, tools and implements provided during the maturing period of the crop;
3) Cash subsistence extended to the settler and his family prior to harvesting;
4) Cost of constructing the settler's house and the development of home lot.

The settlers are expected to repay their debt plus an interest of 6-½ per cent per annum over a period of fifteen years.

The organization of oil palm schemes is similar to that of rubber schemes in all but one important respect. Settlers are not allocated individual holdings but are instead entered into a Register of Holdings in expectation of a share of 10 acres.

On entering the harvesting stage, settlers in oil palm projects are organized into groups of specialists for harvesting, weeding, fertilizing, pest and disease control, cutting the fruit bunches, and carrying the harvested fruit to the road where it will be picked up by the men who load the fruit bunches onto the trucks. Settlers are encouraged to rotate between work assignments so that they learn all jobs. Labor rates are set for each assignment and the settlers are paid accordingly. For approximately two years the settlers' earnings come from these labor payments. When income exceeds operating costs after about two years, dividends are declared. From the dividends FELDA deducts amortization and interest. The settler receives the dividends minus the deductions, which are entered in his financial records. Subsequent dividends are declared at regular intervals in amounts reflecting the market prices for palm oil and palm kernels.

Recently, the system of dividend payments is being replaced by a different system on a trial basis. Under the new system, settlers are organized into groups of twenty men and are assigned to a block of two hundred acres. These twenty men carry out maintenance (weeding and fertilizing) and harvesting jointly, but they are not paid for the labor involved. The production of each group is recorded separately, and each group is paid accordingly. The revenue is shared by the twenty men according to their own arrangement. This system seems to be popular and is gradually being extended to other projects still operating under the first system. Oil palm projects have one feature which distinguishes them from rubber projects. At no stage does the individual receive his own lot. Instead he owns a share in a cooperative. FELDA is aware, however, that the settlers are not all satisfied with this arrangement and that there is a demand for individual holdings. FELDA, therefore, plans to give individual holdings a trial at some future date, but should the trial lead to a lowering of agricultural standards, it is unlikely to be expanded.

In respect to title to land, the land will revert to the State Government after repayment of the FELDA advances, and then the State Government will decide whether to issue one title for a cooperative scheme or to issue titles to individuals.

Obviously, understanding the possession of a title for a share in a cooperative scheme requires considerable sophistication and it tends to confuse the Malay peasantry.

FELDA purchases all produce from the rubber and oil palm schemes at current market prices. It either processes the produce on a non-profit basis or sells the rubber or fruit bunches to commercial processors with the proceeds going directly to the settlers. In 1972, FELDA had only one rubber processing plant for the production of Standard Malaysian Rubber (SMR) and four palm oil mills. In the same year, two Standard Malaysian Rubber factories were under construction and four new palm oil factories. The capital expenses for the factories and mills are met out of loans from the Federal Government or from such other sources as the International Monetary Fund or the Asian Development Bank. The operating expenses, including amortization, are recovered through processing charges taken out of the payments made to the settlers.

Since rubber, palm oil, and palm kernels are all export crops, FELDA has to establish bulk storage facilities at ports within the borders of West Malaysia as a part of the marketing system of the export crops.

Problems

FELDA has run into not insignificant problems in its rubber schemes. Settlers are under obligation to deliver all of their latex production as well as cup-lump rubber and scrap rubber to representatives of FELDA at the collection station. It has, however, become quite obvious that many settlers retain a part of their production, smuggle it out of the projects, and sell it for cash to Chinese merchants. This reduces the rate at which the settlers repay the advances made by FELDA and delays the date of issuance of the title papers. The temptation to sell illegally part of the rubber output is particularly great when the price for rubber is depressed. Rubber delivered on the tenth of the month will not be paid for until a few days after the first of the following month, but the Chinese merchant pays immediately upon delivery of the rubber. This is an especially serious problem in projects made up of six and eight acre lots. FELDA, in fact, no longer considers such small farms as being 'economic.' Low rubber prices have completely upset earlier calculations. To force a settler to forego a substantial portion of his income in order to repay his loan negates both the economic and the social objectives of FELDA.

In the case of the fruit bunches coming from the oil palms, the settlers have no chance to market this part of their production illegally; the merchants in the villages do not have the processing facilities. The whole production is controlled by FELDA.

The second problem for FELDA concerns the strict prohibition of intercropping of subsistence food crops or commercial crops such as tapioca, tobacco, pineapple, or bananas between the rows of rubber trees. Intercropping is a widespread practice among Chinese farmers who earn some money and produce subsistence foodstuff while they are waiting for the trees to mature. In 1968, I saw such farms in various parts of Malaysia. Since the Chinese were applying fertilizer, I saw no evidence of adverse effect on the rubber tree. There was no delay in the date of maturity, but the settlers had to be paid a maintenance allowance until the sixth or seventh year. This meant that the account of a rubber farmer was far greater than that of an oil palm farmer, since the palms begin to produce in the fourth or, at the latest, the fifth year.

In 1968, I visited Mr. Tan, the former director of the Rubber Research Station of Medan, Sumatra, who had migrated to Malaysia and was working on the Research Station of the Guthrie Company. Mr. Tan was trying to convince the Malaysian plantation managers that it was sound and profitable to practice intercropping with catch crops.

My interviews with spokesmen of Harrison and Crosfield, with Guthrie, and with the Rubber Research Institute of Malaysia (RRIM) gave me the definite impression that the planters had an open mind on intercropping of catch crops. Provided the leasehold titles did not rule out intercropping, the plantations were ready to interplant and harvest catch crops. The planters feel that it pays--provided they do not have to pay a conversion premium in return for the permission to shift from a specific crop, such as rubber, to general agriculture. The conversion premium may make intercropping uneconomical or, at least, less attractive.

In 1967, the Rubber Research Institute of Malaysia published an unsigned editorial entitled, "A New Look at Intercropping."[5] After discussing the use of leguminous covercrops, the editorial deals with intercropping of economic plants. The author feels that a new look should be taken at the possibility of replacing leguminous covercrops with marketable crops. He observes that it has long been recognized that the small holder, faced by years of waiting for his rubber to reach the tapping stage, must either use the soil between his immature rubber trees to grow crops that will sustain his family, or he must turn his back on his rubber holding, neglect his rubber and seek a temporary livelihood elsewhere.

Those who oppose intercropping argue that:

1) This practice keeps only an inadequate cover on the ground and hence accelerates soil deterioration and erosion.
2) Constant tillage leads to repeated damage of rubber-tree roots and hence impairs the uptake of nutrients.
3) Intercropping competes excessively with rubber for nutrients.
4) Fertilizer requirements of intensive intercropping can be incompatible with rubber needs.[6]

---

[5]"A New Look at Intercropping," <u>Planters' Bulletin</u> 89 (March 1967).

[6]<u>Ibid</u>.

It must be pointed out that the circle of planters contains numerous practitioners who are not prepared to accept the above cited arguments and forego the harvest of several years.

It is, in my opinion, most unfortunate that FELDA tenaciously clings to an outdated plantation model and rules out the production of such crops as upland rice, corn, tapioca, tobacco, pineapple, bananas, peanuts, beans, and others. There is a market for these commodities, which now have to be imported at considerable expense. As a matter of fact, I would go further and argue that part of the land, now planted in rubber and oil palm, should be used for some of the above-mentioned crops. This would reduce the risks and also spread them over a number of crops.

FELDA should employ agronomists to advise the settlers; the settlers should be given the opportunity to keep their debts down. I was told by a Chinese Member of Parliament that Chinese showed little inclination to apply for admission to FELDA schemes because they resent excessive regimentation.[7] It is quite obvious that Malay villagers are more apt to accept a rule laid down by FELDA than are Chinese villagers --who feel that they can do better by joining other Chinese farmers in establishing new villages that do not place their eggs either in the rubber or in the oil palm basket.

The FELDA system is recommended for settlers without financial resources who by temperament are inclined to follow instructions even when obedience may mean a delay in attaining self-sufficiency and the incurring of larger debts than is necessary. Independent, efficient farmers can do better outside the FELDA schemes. The length of the period of amortization and interest payment cannot be predicted but depends upon the world market price for rubber, palm oil, and palm kernel. Settlers are "locked" into commercial agriculture. I should prefer to see a combination of commercial crops, which can be marketed in Malaysia and Singapore, and export crops to be shipped to distant markets.

---

[7]M.P. from Kulai, Johore, member of the Malaysian-Chinese Association.

APPENDIX A

Table A-1

Percentage Change In Export Volume 1937-1974[1,2]

	Prewar to 1950-52	1950 Decade	1960 Decade	1968-70 to 1972-74	1950-1970	1950-to 1974	Prewar to 1974
Burma	- 66	+ 39	- 54	- 16	- 36	- 46	- 81
Indonesia	+ 18	+ 3	+ 40	+ 74	+ 44	+ 150	+ 196
Malaysia[3]	+ 53	+ 9	+ 61	+ 17	+ 75	+ 105	+ 214
Philippines	+ 9	+ 49	+ 45	+ 37	+116	+ 196	+ 222
Thailand	+ 43	+ 4	+ 53	+ 56	+ 59	+ 148	+ 256

---

[1]Prewar to 1950-52, and 1950-52 to 1958-60 (1950s): International Monetary Fund, International Financial Statistics, (Published jointly by the International Monetary Fund and the International Bank for Reconstruction and Development), various issues, except Malaysia (then Malaya and Singapore). Data for Malaysia from United Nations, Economic Commission for Asia and the Far East, Economic Bulletin for Asia and the Far East, (E/CN.11/ECON.BUL), various issues.

1960s: Burma: United Nations, Department of Economic and Social Affairs, Yearbook of International Trade Statistics, (ST/ESA/STAT/SER.G/23), various issues. Indonesia, Philippines, Thailand: IMF, International Financial Statistics, (see above), various issues. Malaysia: V. V. Bhanoji Rao, The Postwar Development Pattern and Policy of the Malaysian Economy, University of Singapore, Ph.D. Thesis, March 1974, Table B-7.

1968-70 to 1972-74: Data for all countries from IMF, International Financial Statistics, (see above), February 1976.

[2]All percentage changes, except those beginning from prewar base year (1937 for all except Malaysia for which 1938 is used), employ three-year initial and terminal averages, i.e., 1950-52, 1958-60, 1968-70, and 1972-74.

[3]Prewar, 1950-52, and 1958-60 data refer to West Malaysia and Singapore; later data refer to West Malaysia.

Table A-2

Aggregate and Per Capita Product In Constant Prices:
Average Annual Growth Rates[4]

PERIOD	BURMA		INDONESIA		MALAYSIA		PHILIPPINES		SINGAPORE		THAILAND	
	Aggregate	Per Capita	Aggregate	Per Capita	Aggregate	Per Capita	Aggregate	Per Capita	Aggregate	Per Capita	Aggregate	Per Capita
1950-60	5.1	3.9	3.1	1.6	2.5	0	6.0	2.7	NA	NA	5.0	1.9
1960-70	2.3[5]	0.1[5]	3.0	0.4	6.3	3.3	5.2	2.1	9.8	6.2	8.3	5.0
1960-65	NA	NA	1.6	-0.7	6.7	3.7	4.9	1.9	5.5	2.5	7.4	4.1
1965-70	2.3	0.1	5.2	2.1	5.8	2.9	5.6	2.5	13.0	10.9	8.5	5.2
1970-73	2.5	0.2	7.3	4.3	NA	NA	6.1	3.1	12.5	10.5	5.6	2.3

[4] All countries except Malaysia:

1950-60: Douglas S. Paauw, "Economic Progress in Southeast Asia," *Journal of Asian Studies* 23 (November 1963): 69-92.

1960-73: United Nations, *Yearbook of National Accounts Statistics*, (ST/ESA/STAT/SER.0/4), 1974.

Malaysia: V. V. Bhanoji Rao, *National Accounts of West Malaysia, 1947-1971*, (Singapore: Hinemann Educational Books Ltd., 1976), Table B-5, p. 354; and Table B-7, p. 357.

[5] 1962-1970.

APPENDIX B

Table B-1

Percentage Shares of GDP, 1969, 1971, 1973

	Thailand[1]			Malaysia[2]			Indonesia[4]			Philippines[5]		
	1969	1971	1973	1969	1971	1973[3]	1969	1971	1973	1969	1971	1973
Agriculture	35.4	31.1	37.8	33.9	30.1	30.4	49.3	43.6	39.8	36.6	37.2	36.4
Mining	1.9	2.0	1.2	5.6	5.8	5.1	4.7	6.5	9.3	1.8	2.3	2.9
Manufacturing	13.8	15.3	15.1	12.5	13.9	15.4	9.2	9.4	8.7	17.5	19.2	21.3
Construction	7.2	5.6	4.2	3.6	4.0	4.3	2.3	3.4	4.0	3.4	2.5	3.0
Electricity and Water	1.2	1.5	1.4	2.4	2.5	2.4	0.5	0.5	0.5	3.2	3.0	2.9
Transport and Communications	6.6	7.1	6.3	4.2	4.4	3.9	2.3	4.3	4.0	0.5	0.6	0.5
Trade	11.9	13.8	14.2	13.9	13.9	13.5	17.5	18.8	20.4	9.5	9.5	9.4
Banking, Insurance, etc.	4.0	4.6	4.3	1.9	2.1	2.1	0.8	1.2	1.2	4.5	4.9	4.7
Ownership of Dwellings	2.1	2.2	1.7	4.4	4.4	3.8	2.0	1.9	2.0	4.9	4.4	3.8
Public Adminstration	4.9	5.2	4.3	6.2	7.1	7.3	5.0	5.6	6.1	7.6	7.1	6.0
Other Services	10.9	11.6	9.5	10.7	11.2	11.2	5.4	4.8	4.0	10.4	9.5	9.0

[1] National Economic and Social Development Board, current factor costs.

[2] Department of Statistics, current factor costs.

[3] Economic Planning Unit estimate.

[4] Central Bureau of Statistics, at current market prices.

[5] National Economic Development Authority, current factor costs.

Table B-2

GNP and GNP Per Capita, 1972/3 - 1974/5[6]

		1972/3	1973/4	1974/5
Thailand	GNP (US$ mil.)	7,992	9,364	12,205
	GNP per capita (US$)	199	227	287
Malaysia	GNP (US$ mil.)	4,241	5,408	8,167
	GNP per capita (US$)	369	458	539
Indonesia (GDP)	GDP (US$ mil.)	11,807	17,108	25,542
	GDP per capita (US$)	163	175	190
Philippines	GNP (US$ mil.)	9,015	12,461	15,018
	GNP per capita (US$)	225	309	367

[6] *Far Eastern Economic Review Yearbook 1976*, pp. 307, 219, 188, 263. For Indonesia the figures given are for GDP.

Table B-3

Central Government Capital or
Development Expenditures (US$ mil.)

	Thailand[7]		Malaysia[8]		Indonesia[9]		Philippines[10]	
	FY 1969	FY 1975	FY 1969	FY 1974	FY 1970/1	FY 1975/6	FY 1969/70	FY 1972/3
Agriculture (incl. Irrigation)	63.7	75.7	66.0	203.0	84	689	8.4	58.6
Industry and Mining	3.6	2.3	12.7	122.0	5	115	2.5	0.4
Power	4.7	0.1	4.7	173.0	19	114	--	--
Transport and Communications	127.7	146.0	22.7	30.8	47	255	63.6	104.0
Education	51.8	77.5	14.3	78.0	23	270	9.7	9.3
Health	6.6	9.2	6.0	26.0	9	34	3.2	3.2
Water and Sewerage	8.4	11.7	--	--	--	--	--	--
Other	36.6	106.8	52.3	130.0	142	1,876	19.7	138.5
Total Capital/ Development	308	440	191	765	329	3,353	107	314
Total Expenditures	1,158	2,178	629	1,471	691	6,712	598	1,171

[7] Bank of Thailand, estimate 1975.

[8] Ministry of Finance--water included in Power, defense in Other.

[9] Ministry of Finance, estimate 1975/6.

[10] National Budget Commission.

Table B-4

Proportional Expenditures on GDP (At Current Prices)[11]

	Thailand		Malaysia		Indonesia		Philippines	
	1971	1973	1971	1973	1971	1973[12]	1971	1973
Consumption	79.2	74.1	80.4	75.3	87.4	82.4	81.3	76.3
Private	67.5	64.2	60.5	55.8	78.4	71.6	72.6	68.1
Public	11.7	9.9	19.9	19.5	9.0	10.8	8.7	8.2
Capital Formation	22.5	20.6	17.4	17.9	15.3	18.3	18.5	17.7
Private	15.3	15.6	10.6	9.2	--	--	--	--
Public	7.2	5.0	6.8	8.7	--	--	--	--
Change in Stock	1.4	6.9	1.1	--	--	--	2.0	2.2
Exports	17.3	19.9	42.1	44.7	13.4	18.0	17.6	22.5
(Less) Imports	20.4	21.5	40.9	38.2	16.0	18.8	18.3	19.0
GDP (US$ mil)	7,270	10,710	4,091	6,788	9,984	15,916	7,468	10,485
Population (mil)	37.4	39.8	11.5	11.8	119	122	37.9	40.2
Population Growth Rate[13]	3.0	2.8	2.6	2.7	2.1	2.5	2.9	3.0
GDP Per Capita (US$)	194	269	356	575	84	155	197	261

[11] World Bank Estimates.

[12] Provisional, see Appendix B-2.

[13] Yearly, from previous year.

Table B-5

Central Government Revenues (US$ Mil.)

	Thailand[14]		Malaysia[15]		Indonesia[16]		Philippines[17]	
	FY 1969	est.FY 1975	FY 1969	Budget 1974	FY 1972/73	est. 1975/76	FY 1969	Prelim. 1972/73
Total	1,158	2,178	629	1,471	1,770	6,617		
Non Tax								
Other	76	211	120	179 }	1,450[18]	6,180[18]		
Extra Budgetary	29	8						
Foreign Grants	73	34	8.3	3.3 }	360[19]	575		
Net External Borrowing	- 2	- 1	57	76.7				
Domestic Financing	151	223	126	477				
Tax	831	1,702	570	1,281	1,370	5,905	479	1,002
Direct Income	99	290	180	440	726	4,528	146	289
Petroleum Royalties				11	477[20]	3,739[20]		
Consumption	293	736	61	189	303	458	83	108
Fiscal Monopolies	30							
Other							123	192
International Trade	350	518	220	424	341	920	106	279
on Imports	265	410	175	311	185	533	90	212
on Exports	84	108	93	113	24	173	16	67
Rice	70	62	--	--				
Rubber	11	20	39	34				
Other	3	26	13	36				
Tin	--	--	41	42				

---

[14]Bank of Thailand.

[15]Ministry of Finance.

[16]Ministry of Finance.

[17]Bureau of Internal Revenue, Bureau of Customs.

[18]Includes "domestic revenues."

[19]"Development Funds," counterpart, and project aid.

[20]Corporate tax on oil.

Table B-6

Balance of Payments (US$ Mil.)

	Exports fob	Imports cif	Non-Factor Net Services	Net Capital Investment	Balance	Oil Net
Thailand[21]						
1972	1,046	-1,473	332	271	176	
1973	1,532	-2,062	356	216	42	
1974	2,438	-3,165	405	722	400	
1975(est.)	2,440	-3,475	375	560	-100	
Malaysia[22]						
1970	2,127	-1,722	-623	275	57	
1971	2,065	-1,809	-669	538	125	
1972	1,997	-1,879	-771	744	91	
1973	2,920	-2,287	-855	727	505	
1974	4,241	-4,173	-533		269(?)	
Indonesia[23]						
1971/2	784	-1,249	-187	354	-100	204
1972/3	974	-1,661	-269	45	-425	399
1973/4	1,905	-2,938	-364	391	-360	641
1974/5(est.)	2,060	-4,456	-493	202	-270	2,638
1975/6(est.)	1,968	-5,390	-670	620	-403	3,069
Philippines[24]						
1970	1,083	-1,090	-141	181	33	
1971	1,149	-1,186	- 88	124	- 1	
1972	1,109	-1,260	- 26	174	- 3	
1973	1,871	-1,597	- 30	210	454	
1974	2,725	-3,143	- 65	270	-212	
1975	3,140	-3,960	-110	280	-650	
1976,proj.	3,310	-4,560	-120	300	-1,070	

[21] Bank of Thailand.

[22] Department of Statistics.

[23] Bank of Indonesia.

[24] International Monetary Fund and Central Bank of the Philippines.

Table B-7

Employment (in Thousands of Workers and by Per Cent of Work Force)

	Thailand[25]				Malaysia[26]				Indonesia[27]		Philippines[28]			
	1960	(%)	1970	(%)	1965	(%)	1970	(%)	1971	(%)	1960	(%)	1973	(%)
Agriculture	11,332	82.0	13,202	79.0	1,350	52.1	1,454	49.3	30,550	7.1	5,224	61.2	7,016	52.9
Mining	30	.2	87	.5	66	2.5	64	2.2	80	.2	29	.3	62	.5
Manufacturing	470	3.0	683	4.0		8.4	270	9.2	1,550	3.8	1,036	12.1	1,418	.7
Construction	69	.5	182	1.0	90	3.5	103	3.3	600	1.5	231	2.7	522	3.9
Utilities	16	.1	25	.1	16	.6	19	.6	--	--	20	.2	37	.3
Commerce	779	6.0	876	5.0	287	11.1	340	11.6	3,600	8.8	753	8.8	1,660	13.5
Transport and Communications	166	1.0	268	1.6	101	3.9	110	3.7	850	2.2	271	3.2	505	3.6
Services	654	5.0	184	7.0	463	17.9	580	19.7	3,900	9.5	929	11.0	2,012	15.2
Unknown	234	2.0	146	.8	--	--	--	--	--	--	46	.5	29	.2
Total	13,749	--	16,652	--	2,590	--	2,940	--	41,130	--	8,539	--	13,262	--

[25] Census reports 1960, 1970. The latter is regarded as particularly unreliable.

[26] Second Malaysia Plan.

[27] Central Statistical Bureau; figures an average between agricultural "on" and "off" seasons.

[28] Bureau of Census and Statistics surveys.

Table B-8

Principal Gross Commodity Exports (US$ Mil.)[29]

	Thailand[30]			Malaysia[31]			Indonesia[32]			Philippines[33]		
	1965	1971	1974	1965(66)	1971	1974	1965(67)	1971	1974	1965	1971	1974
Rice	216.7	145.5	488.9	--	--	--	--	--	--	--	--	--
Rubber	100.0	95.3	251.8	487.3	486.7	1,201.0	223.1	222.3	496	--	--	--
Maize	48.5	114.3	303.9	--	--	--	--	--	--	--	--	--
Tin	20.0	78.5	154.8	290.7	302.0	586.7	37.9	64.0	142	--	--	--
Tapioca Products	33.8	62.0	191.8	--	--	--	--	--	--	--	--	--
Kenaf and Jute	55.1	46.8	42.3	--	--	--	--	--	--	--	--	--
Sugar	5.0	19.1	187.9	--	--	--	--	--	--	147	220	739
Shrimp	5.5	12.4	32.1	--	--	--	--	--	--	--	--	--
Forest Products	10.1	9.2	20.1	120.0	280.0	530.0	6.0	169.0	747	195	264	246
Palm Oil	--	--	--	35.7	126.7	425.8	27.3	46.0	136	--	--	--
Pineapple Products	--	--	--	(14.7)	13.6	16.3	--	--	--	12	20	NA[34]
Petroleum and Products	--	--	--	29.0	130.0	280.0	271.9	478.0	2,700	6	24	NA
Iron	--	--	--	(45.4)	6.9	1.3	--	--	--	--	--	--
Copper	--	--	--	--	--	--	--	--	--	47	185	393
Pepper	--	--	--	(16.8)	22.0	42.1	(18.0)	24.0	38	--	--	--
Chromate Ore	--	--	--	--	--	--	--	--	--	11	6	NA
Copra	--	--	--	(6.1)	4.6	NA	18.0	15.0	NA	170	114	139
Palm Kernels	--	--	--	(3.1)	2.6	NA	4.0	6.0	6	--	--	--
Coconut Oil	--	--	--	(7.3)	12.4	19.6	--	--	--	68	103	380
Bauxite	--	--	--	--	5.7	--	NA	NA	NA	--	--	--
Tea	--	--	--	--	--	--	16.9	28.9	NA	--	--	--
Tobacco and Products	--	--	--	--	--	--	18.7	20.0	37	16	15	NA
Total Principal Exports	495.0	583.0	1,674.0	1,053.0	1,388.0	3,138.0	?	788.0	3,656	443	747	1,897
Total Exports	622.0	831.0	2,512.0	--	1,652.0	3,992.0	?	1,270.0	4,309	745.4	114.8	--

[29] Note: Tabulated values in parenthesis refer to the years in parenthesis at the column head.

[30] Bank of Thailand.

[31] Malaysian Department of Statistics.

[32] Bank of Indonesia.

[33] Central Bank of the Philippines.

[34] NA = Not Available.

SOUTHEAST ASIA PROGRAM
CENTER FOR INTERNATIONAL STUDIES
OHIO UNIVERSITY
ATHENS, OHIO 45701

ORDER FROM:
Ohio University Press
Administrative Annex
Ohio University
Athens, Ohio 45701

Out of print volumes can be obtained in Xerox or microfilm format through the Inter-Library Loan Department, Alden Library, Ohio University, Athens, Ohio 45701.

Publication Number:

1 - TREASURES AND TRIVIA: Doctoral Dissertations on Southeast Asia Accepted by Universities in the United States. Compiled by Lian The and Paul W. van der Veur. 1968. 155 pp. $5.00

2 - PUBLIC PROTEST IN INDONESIA. By Ann Ruth Willner. 1968. 21 pp. $1.75

3 - DEVELOPMENTAL CHALLENGE IN MALAYSIA. By Siew Nim Chee. 1968. 22 pp. $1.75

4 - THE USE OF HISTORY. By Wang Gungwu. 1968. 24 pp. $1.75

5 - THE TRADITIONAL USE OF THE FORESTS IN MAINLAND SOUTHEAST ASIA. By James L. Cobban. *Out of print.*

6 - CONFLICT AND POLITICAL DEVELOPMENT IN SOUTHEAST ASIA: An Exploration in the International Implications of Comparative Theory. By Gerald S. Maryanov. *Out of print.*

7 - SRI PADUKA: The Exile of the Prince of Ayondha. Translated by S.M. Ponniah. *Out of print.*

8 - AGRARIAN UNREST IN THE PHILIPPINES: Guardia de Honor -- Revitalization within the Revolution; Rizalistas -- Contemporary Revitalization Movements in the Philippines. By David R. Sturtevant. 1969. 1973 reprint. 44 pp. $2.75

9 - PANDANGGO-SA-ILAW: The Politics of Occidental Mindoro. By Remigio E. Agpalo. 1969. 32 pp. $2.00

10 - REPRESSION AND REVOLT: The Origins of the 1948 Communist Insurrection in Malaya and Singapore. By Michael R. Stenson. *Out of print.*

11 - RUBBER AND THE MALAYSIAN ECONOMY: Implications of Declining Prices. By Tan Sri Lim Swee Aun. 1969. 36 pp. $2.50

12 - EDUCATION AND SOCIAL CHANGE IN COLONIAL INDONESIA: I. Progress and Procrastination in Education in Indonesia prior to World War II; II. The Social and Geographical Origins of Dutch-Educated Indonesians. By Paul W. van der Veur. 1969. 62 pp. $3.50

13 - COMMUNAL VIOLENCE IN MALAYSIA 1969: The Political Aftermath. By Felix V. Gagliano. *Out of print.*

14 - SOVIET AND AMERICAN AID TO INDONESIA 1949-1968. By Usha Mahajani. *Out of print.*

15 - POLITICS AMONG BURMANS: A Study of Intermediary Leaders. By John Badgley. 1970. 1973 reprint. 125 pp. $4.50

16 - TRADE AND EMPIRE IN MALAYA AND SINGAPORE, 1869-1874. By D.R. SarDesai. 1970. 22 pp. $1.75

17 - EXPANSION OF THE VIETNAM WAR INTO CAMBODIA: Action and Response by the Governments of North Vietnam, South Vietnam, Cambodia, and the United States. By Peter A. Poole. 1970. 70 pp. $3.50

Publication Number:

18 - THE PRE-WORLD WAR II PERANAKAN CHINESE PRESS OF JAVA: A Preliminary Survey. By Leo Suryadinata. 1971. 44 pp. $2.75

19 - A REVIEW OF COMMUNITY-ORIENTED ECOLOGICAL RESEARCH IN THE PHILIPPINES. By Robert A. Bullington. *Out of print.*

20 - A BIBLIOGRAPHY OF PHILIPPINE LINGUISTICS. By Nobleza C. Asuncion-Landé. *Out of print.*

21 - THE BURMA-YUNNAN RAILWAY: Anglo-French Rivalry in Mainland Southeast Asia and South China, 1895-1902. By J. Chandran. *Out of print.*

22 - THE NORTH BORNEO CHARTERED COMPANY'S ADMINISTRATION OF THE BAJAU, 1878-1909: The Pacification of a Maritime, Nomadic People. By James F. Warren. *Out of print.*

23 - PROMINENT INDONESIAN CHINES IN THE TWENTIETH CENTURY: A Preliminary Survey. By Leo Suryadinata. *Out of print.*

24 - PEACOCKS, PAGODAS, AND PROFESSOR HALL: A Critique of the Persisting Use of Historiography as an Apology for British Empire-Building in Burma. By Manuel Sarkisyanz. 1972. 68 pp. $3.50

25 - IMBALANCES IN DEVELOPMENT: The Indonesian Experience. By Selo Soemardjan. 1972. 26 pp. $2.00

26 - THE VERHANDELINGEN VAN HET BATAVIAASCH GENOOTSCHAP: An Annotated Content Analysis. Compiled by Lian The and Paul W. van der Veur. 1973. 150 pp., Index. $5.00

27 - JAPAN'S SCHEME FOR THE LIBERATION OF BURMA: The Role of the *Minami Kikan* and the "Thirty Comrades." By Won Z. Yoon. 1973. 65 pp., Bib. $3.50

28 - EDUCATIONAL SPONSORSHIP BY ETHNICITY: A Preliminary Analysis of the West Malaysian Experience. By Yoshimitsu Takei, John C. Bock, and Bruce Saunders. 1973. 44 pp. $3.00

29 - BLOOD, BELIEVER, AND BROTHER: The Development of Voluntary Associations in Malaysia. By Stephen A. Douglas and Paul Pederson. 1973. 119 pp., App. $4.50

30 - THE DYNAMICS OF POLITICS AND ADMINISTRATION IN RURAL THAILAND. By Clark D. Neher. *Out of print.*

31 - PEASANT CITIZENS: Politics, Religion, and Modernization in Kelantan, Malaysia. By Manning Nash. 1974. 179 pp., Bib. 1977 reprint. $7.00

32 - MARGINAL MAN IN A COLONIAL SOCIETY: Abdoel Moeis' *Salah Asuhan*. By David de Queljoe. 1974. 43 pp. $3.00

33 - THE NEUTRALIZATION OF SOUTHEAST ASIA: An Analysis of the Malaysian/ASEAN Proposal. By Marvin C. Ott. 1974. 57 pp. $3.50

34 - THE LAND-TO-THE-TILLER PROGRAM AND RURAL RESOURCE MOBILIZATION IN THE MEKONG DELTA OF SOUTH VIETNAM. By C. Stuart Callison. 1974. 48 pp. $3.00

35 - THE FUTURE OF BURMA IN PERSPECTIVE: A Symposium. Edited and with an Introduction by Josef Silverstein. 1974. 104 pp. $4.50

36 - INDOCHINA: PERSPECTIVES FOR RECONCILIATION. Edited and with an Introduction by Peter A. Poole. 1975. 92 pp. $4.25

Publication Number:

37 - THE COMINTERN AND VIETNAMESE COMMUNISM. By William J. Duiker. 1975. 48 pp. $3.25

38 - BROKER, MEDIATOR, PATRON AND KINSMAN: An Historical Analysis of Key Leadership Roles in a Rural Malaysian District. By Connor Bailey. 1976. 89 pp., Bib. LC75-620141. $4.25

39 - CHIEF EXECUTIVES IN BLACK AFRICA AND SOUTHEAST ASIA: A Descriptive Analysis of Social Background and Characteristics. By Edward Baum and Felix Gagliano. 1976. 43 pp., App. $3.00

40 - FREEMASONRY IN INDONESIA FROM RADERMACHER TO SOEKANTO, 1762-1961. By Paul W. van der Veur. 1976. 42 pp., App. $3.25

41 - CULTURAL-ECOLOGICAL PERSPECTIVES ON SOUTHEAST ASIA: A Symposium. Edited and introduced by William Wood. 1977. 192 pp. LC76-620062. ISBN 0-8214-0322-2. $8.00

42 - SOUTHEAST ASIA, AN EMERGING CENTER OF WORLD INFLUENCE? ECONOMIC AND RESOURCE CONSIDERATIONS. Edited and introduced by Wayne Raymond and K. Mulliner. Comments and Conclusions by Laurence D. Stifel. 1977. 136 pp. LC 76-620090. ISBN 0-8214-0324-9. $6.00

43 - POLLUTION AND POLITICS IN THE PHILIPPINES. By Ross Marlay. 1977. 131 pp. LC 76-620091. ISBN 0-8214-0325-7. $6.00

ALSO distributors for:

INTERNATIONAL BIOGRAPHICAL DIRECTORY OF SOUTHEAST ASIA SPECIALISTS. Compiled by Robert O. Tilman. 1969. 373 pp. Special price: $1.25

A collection of about 1,000 vitae of Southeast Asia specialists throughout the world preceded by an introductory analysis of the data collected. The study was undertaken as a project by the Inter-University Southeast Asia Committee of the Association for Asian Studies.

SEARCH FOR NEW GUINEA'S BOUNDARIES: From Torres Strait to the Pacific By Paul W. Van der Veur. ANU Press, 1966. 176 pp. $10.00

AFRICA PROGRAM
CENTER FOR INTERNATIONAL STUDIES
OHIO UNIVERSITY
ATHENS, OHIO 45701

ORDER FROM:
Ohio University Press
Administrative Annex
Ohio University
Athens, Ohio 45701

Out of print volumes can be obtained in Xerox or microfilm format through the Inter-Library Loan Department, Alden Library, Ohio University, Athens, Ohio 45701.

Publication Number:

1 - THE NEW ENGLISH OF THE ONITSHA CHAPBOOKS. By Harold Reeves Collins. 1968. 22 pp. $1.75

2 - DIRECTIONS IN GHANAIAN LINGUISTICS: A Brief Survey. By Paul F.A. Kotey. 1969. 20 pp. $1.75

3 - DEFINING NATIONAL PURPOSE IN LESOTHO. By Richard F. Weisfelder. 1961. 39 pp. $2.25

4 - RECENT AGRICULTURAL CHANGE EAST OF MOUNT KENYA. By Frank E. Bernard. 1969. 41 pp. $2.75

5 - THE STRUGGLE AGAINST SLEEPING SICKNESS IN NYASALAND AND NORTHERN RHODESIA, 1900-1922. By Norman H. Pollock. 1969. 21 pp. $1.75

6 - BOTSWANA AND ITS SOUTHERN NEIGHBOR: The Patterns of Linkage and the Options in Statecraft. By Richard Dale. *Out of print.*

7 - WOLF COURTS GIRL: The Equivalence of Hunting and Mating in Bushman Thought. By Daniel F. McCall. 1970. 24 pp. $1.75

8 - MARKERS IN ENGLISH-INFLUENCED SWAHILI CONVERSATION. By Carol M. Eastman. 1970. 25 pp. $2.00

9 - THE TERRITORIAL EXPANSION OF THE NANDI OF KENYA, 1500-1905. By Bob J. Walter. 1970. 37 pp. $3.00

10 - SOME GEOGRAPHICAL ASPECTS OF WEST AFRICAN DEVELOPMENT. By R.J. Harrison Church. 1970. 34 pp. $2.75

11 - THE IMPACT OF THE PROTÉGÉ SYSTEM IN MOROCCO, 1800-1912. By Leland Bowie. 1970. 21 pp. $1.75

12 - MARKET DEVELOPMENT IN TRADITIONALLY MARKETLESS SOCIETIES: A Perspective on East Africa. By Charles M. Good. 1971. 39 pp. $3.00

13 - SOUTH AFRICA'S OUTWARD STRATEGY: A Foreign Policy Dilemma for the United States. By Larry W. Bowman. 1971. 1973 reprint. 32 pp. $2.50

14 - BANTU EDUCATION AND THE EDUCATION OF AFRICANS IN SOUTH AFRICA. By R. Hunt Davis, Jr. 1972. 60 pp. $3.50

15 - TOWARD A THEORY OF THE AFRICAN UPPER STRATUM IN SOUTH AFRICA. By Thomas E. Nyquist. 1972. 66 pp. $3.50

16 - THE BASOTHO MONARCHY: A Spent Force or a Dynamic Political Factor? By Richard F. Weisfelder. 1972. 106 pp. $4.00

17 - YORUBA PROVERBS: Translation and Annotation. By Bernth Lindfors and Oyekan Owomoyela. 1973. 86 pp. $4.00

Publication Number:

18 - POST-MILITARY COUP STRATEGY IN UGANDA: Amin's Early Attempts to Consolidate Political Support. By Jeffrey T. Strate. 1973. 65 pp. $3.75

19 - HIGHLAND MOSAIC: A Critical Anthology of Ethiopian Literature in English. Compiled by Paul E. Huntsberger. 1973. 133 pp. $4.75

20 - THE KENYA NATIONAL YOUTH SERVICE: A Governmental Response to Young Political Activists. By Richard L. Coe. 1973. 39 pp. $2.50

21 - CONSTRAINTS ON THE EXPANSION OF COMMERCIAL AGRICULTURE: Iringa District, Tanzania. By Marilyn Silberfein. 1974. 59 pp. $3.50

22 - ECHO AND CHORUSES: "Ballad of the Cells: and Selected Shorter Poems. By Cosmo Pieterse. 1974. 75 pp. $3.75

23 - THE NIGER-NIGERIAN BOUNDARY, 1890-1906: A Study of Ethnic Frontiers and a Colonial Boundary. By Derrick J. Thom. 1975. 49 pp. $3.25

24 - A COMPREHENSIVE PERIODICAL BIBLIOGRAPHY OF NIGERIA, 1960-1970. Compiled by Edward Baum. 1975. 261 pp. $6.00

25 - ABYSSINIA TO ZONA AL SUR DEL DRAA: A Guide to the Political Units of Africa in the Period 1950-1974. Second Edition. By Eugene C. Kirchherr. 1975. 50 pp. $3.50

26 - THE ORIGINS AND DEVELOPMENT OF EFIK SETTLEMENTS IN SOUTHEASTERN NIGERIA. By Kannan K. Nair, 1975. 42 pp. $3.00

27 - MOUNTAIN WARRIORS: The Pre-Colonial Meru of Mt. Kenya. By Jeffrey Fadiman. 1976. 82 pp., Bib. $4.00

28 - DEPENDENCE AND UNDERDEVELOPMENT: The Development and Foreign Politics of Zambia. By Timothy M. Shaw. 1976. 67 pp., Bib. $3.75

29 - CHIEF EXECUTIVES IN BLACK AFRICA AND SOUTHEAST ASIA: A Descriptive Analysis of Social Background and Characteristics. By Edward Baum and Felix Gagliano. 1976. 43 pp., App. $3.00

30 - FEARS AND WORRIES OF NIGERIAN IGBO SECONDARY SCHOOL STUDENTS: An Empirical Psycho-Cultural Study. By Sadek H. Samaan and Anne J. Samaan. 1976. 90 pp., App., Bib. $4.50

ALSO: WEST/AFRICAN PIDGIN-ENGLISH: A Descriptive Linguistic Analysis with Texts and Glossary from the Cameroon Area. By Gilbert D. Schneider. 1969. 256 pp. $6.00

This book is an attempt to apply the basic principles of structural linguistics to West African Pidgin-English. After an introductory chapter which deals with the general characteristics of the language as spoken in the Cameroon area, the author proceeds to the treatment of sounds, meaningful units, and sentence patterns. A glossary and bibliography are included.